AMELIA, THE FLYING SQUIRREL

and Other Great Stories of God's Smallest Creatures

Other books in the series
The Good Lord Made Them All
by Joe L. Wheeler

Owney, the Post Office Dog
and Other Great Dog Stories

Dick, the Babysitting Bear
and Other Great Wild Animal Stories

Smoky, the Ugliest Cat in the World
and Other Great Cat Stories

Spot, the Dog That Broke the Rules
and Other Great Heroic Animal Stories

Wildfire, the Red Stallion
and Other Great Horse Stories

AMELIA, THE FLYING SQUIRREL

and Other Great Stories of God's Smallest Creatures

Compiled and edited by
Joe L. Wheeler

PACIFIC PRESS® PUBLISHING ASSOCIATION
NAMPA, IDAHO
OSHAWA, ONTARIO, CANADA
WWW.PACIFICPRESS.COM

Cover art by Lars Justinen
Cover designed by Justinen Creative Group
Interior illustrations from the library of Joe L. Wheeler
Inside design by Aaron Troia

The author assumes full responsibility for the accuracy of all facts and quotations as cited in this book.

Additional copies of this book are available by calling toll-free 1-800-765-6955 or by visiting www.adventistbookcenter.com

www.joewheelerbooks.com

Representing the author is WordServe Literary Group Ltd., 10152 Knoll Circle, Highland Ranch, CO 80130

Library of Congress Cataloging-in-Publication Data:

Amelia, the flying squirrel : and other great stories of God's smallest creatures / compiled and edited by Joe L. Wheeler.
p. cm.—(The Good Lord made them all)
ISBN 13: 978-0-8163-2366-1 (pbk.)
ISBN 10: 0-8163-2366-6 (pbk.)
1. Animals—Anecdotes. I. Wheeler, Joe L., 1936-
QL791.A445 2009
241'.693—dc22

2009023742

09 10 11 12 13   5 4 3 2 1

DEDICATION

Though our animal story collections are loved and read by all age groups, from the youngest to the oldest, nevertheless there is one audience more important than any other: and that is children. For studies reveal that if children fail to fall in love with reading by the third grade, they are then almost certain to grow up as nonreaders.

The secret, of course, is for parents to first read aloud to their children, beginning at a very early age—indeed some begin while the child is still in the womb. Children who are read aloud to from an early age soon learn to love reading on their own.

Our daughter, Michelle, and her husband, Duane, have carried on this tradition with their two sons. And when we're with them, Connie and I read to our grandsons every opportunity we get. For are they not our future? Is it possible one of them will grow up to be a story anthologizer like his grandpa? Only time will tell.

Therefore, it is fitting that I dedicate this sixth animal collection to two exceedingly lively, rambunctious, curious, and fascinating boys of eleven and eight who, though all boy, remain tender and empathetic—our beloved grandsons:

TAYLOR CULMORE
and
SETH CULMORE
of Annapolis, Maryland

CONTENTS

INTRODUCTION

QUESTIONS HELP ME KNOW THINGS

Joseph Leininger Wheeler

"Daddy, can we go for a walk along the creek?"

"I guess so [regretfully laying down the book I wanted to read]. Go tell Mama so she won't worry about where you are."

And so we go.

* * * * *

"Daddy, what's *that*?"

"What's *what*?"

"The thing that's trying to get into that flower?"

"Oh, that's just a bee."

"What's it doing? Oh look! It moved to another flower."

"It's sucking up nectar."

"What's 'nectar'?"

"Oh, it's kind of like sugar."

"I like sugar too. . . . Oh, look! What's that thing that jumped out of the water?"

"Just a fish."

"What kind of a fish?"

"I don't know. . . . I didn't see it that well."

"Why did it jump out of the water?"

"Why? Uh . . . uh . . . maybe it saw a bug flying over the water and decided to eat it for breakfast."

"Yuck."

"Oh, Daddy, what's that thing that just jumped?"

"What thing?"

"*There,* Daddy, that greenish thing—oh, see, it jumped again!"

"That's a frog."

"What's a frog?"

"Oh, it's, uh, kind of a small animal that likes to live where it's wet."

"I like to get wet too—but not in a bathtub. . . . What do frogs do?"

"Oh, they eat lots and lots of bugs."

"Is that all they do?"

"How should I know?"

"But you *must* know. You know *everything,* Daddy."

"Don't I wish. . . . They, uh, just like to hop around in wet grass and bushes . . . swim in the water, and sleep. They seem to sleep a lot."

"Oh. Daddy, what kind of bird is that?"

"What bird?"

"*That* one. The one in that tree by the big rock—see it's got red on its wing."

"Oh, that's a red-winged blackbird."

"What's it doing?"

"*Doing?* I don't know. I guess it's hungry too and looking for breakfast."

"What kind of breakfast?"

"Oh, probably bugs."

"Poor bird."

"Oh, look! Look at that be-yootiful thing over there! What *is* it?"

"That? Oh, that's a dragonfly."

"Doesn't look like a dragon to me. Why is it called a dragonfly, Daddy?"

"Huh? I don't know."

"But you've *got* to know, Daddy."

"Well, Greg, it doesn't look much like a dragon, does it?"

"No. So why is it called a 'dragonfly'?"

[*Groan*]. "I guess we'll have to find out. We'll look it up in the encyclopedia when we get home."

"Promise?"

"I promise. . . ."

"Oh, look, Daddy, what's *that?*"

"Greg, you're driving me crazy with all your questions!"

"But Daddy—questions help me *know* things!"

* * * * *

When our son Greg was small, he unleashed on us a nonstop barrage of questions. Indeed, they came so fast, they left us exhausted. How could one little boy contain so many? And when I finally blew my top, he stopped me in my proverbial tracks with a line that lives on in family history: "But Daddy—questions help me *know* things!"

A sense of wonder

Each child is born with this God-given sense of wonder—an insatiable yearning to know. It is the tragedy of our age that so many parents slowly but surely stifle their child's excitement about the world and the creatures that live in it. Saying "I'm too busy" so often that the child finally ceases to ask the questions that could provide meaningful growth, and instead veers into substitutions that, more often than not, are destructive and debilitating.

About this collection

Where our books are concerned, I take nothing for granted. Nor am I willing to accept anything less than the very best. Each of the books in this series (*Owney, Smoky, Wildfire, Dick,* and *Spot*) are the best we could put together, so I desired no less for our sixth collection. As has been happening more and more often in recent years, our readers continue to be ahead of me. Three times during the past year, readers have told me, "Do the next one on small creatures." Two suggested, "Do one on rodents." Clearly, they felt that the logical successor to dogs, cats, horses, wild animals, and animal heroes, would be "God's smaller creatures."

Having said that, however, my publishing partners no longer feel it necessary to even have a theme. As long as the lead story and cover illustration is gripping enough, that's all it seems to take. It has been interesting to watch browsers eddy past our book-signing tables. I don't believe there's a child in America who could walk past all five without pausing.

This particular collection did present unforeseen problems, not least of which, *How do you individualize animal personality traits if the creature being portrayed is too small to evidence such things?* In some cases, I've had to substitute description for story plot. Nevertheless, I believe you'll continue to find the overall mix just as fascinating as those that preceded it. I'll go even further: I wouldn't be at all surprised to see this collection become one of the most popular of all, for I can't ever remember reading in one book so many stories of such diverse creatures.

Now that it appears this animal series has no intention of fading away in the near future, it is time to point out three current authors who are helping to anchor these collections. Linda Franklin of Chetwyn, British Columbia, returns with another memorable bird story. P. J. Platz (Patricia and Traci Lambrecht of Stillwater, Minnesota), returns for the third time. And Penny Porter of Tucson, Arizona—what would we do without her! Her stories have graced every book so far. The other authors appear for the first time. We'll be interested in your responses, which ones you like best, and why.

CODA

I look forward to hearing from you! I always welcome the stories, responses, and suggestions that are sent to us from our readers. I am putting together collections centered on other genres as well. You may reach me by writing to:

Joe L. Wheeler, PhD
P.O. Box 1246
Conifer, CO 80433

* * * * *

"Questions Help Me Know Things," by Joseph Leininger Wheeler. Copyright © 2009. Printed by permission of the author.

BUT, GRANDPA, THEY'RE SO *CUTE*!
Mama Cottontail and the Big Bad Gopher Snake

Steve Hamilton

It was a warm day in May, and I was hanging out with Grandpa, my very best friend. I was sitting on his lap on the second-story porch of the creek house where my grandparents lived in the hills overlooking California's Napa Valley. They called it "the creek house" because the backyard sloped right down to a beautiful creek. From where we were sitting, we could see across the yard down to the water.

Grandpa and Grandma also owned a 640-acre ranch on the very top of Howell Mountain, about five miles away, but since the mountaintop house wasn't finished yet, they were still living below in Angwin.

Grandpa and I had been working awfully hard for the past month. He had been using his axe, saw, shovel, rake, and biggest hoe, clearing buckbrush, manzanita, blackberry vines, small trees and weeds, and placing them in burn piles. I helped by lugging the tools over to him as needed and dragging the smaller limbs and branches over to the piles. Grandpa let me use his homemade torch to help light the piles.

"Whoa, stand back!" he commanded. "These are really hot fires!"

I couldn't wait to tell my dad about this. To a boy who would be three years old in two weeks, this was high adventure. My grandpa made me feel so important, I was about to pop the buttons on my striped bib overalls: "We made this huge farm and planted this garden all by ourselves, didn't we, Grandpa?"

Though it was less than an acre, I considered it to be a large ranch.

"Yes, Stevie, we did it *all* by ourselves."

While we were sitting there looking over our new farm, Grandma brought us two green apples and some soft peanut butter and melted caramel all mixed up. She sure knew what I liked best. Grandpa sliced the apples, and we dipped them into the gooey stuff, and it was straight from heaven.

That afternoon we were celebrating because the garden was finished at last: it was all planted and the seeds we had planted several weeks before had sprouted and were starting to grow. I could almost taste the green peas, lettuce, corn on the cob, tomatoes, spinach, and squash. My parents had taught me to love fresh veggies—and I could hardly wait.

I climbed down off Grandpa's lap and was proudly staring out across the rows and rows of vegetables we had planted. Some of the sprouts were already almost two inches tall. Suddenly, from under the far brushy thicket, out came a mama cottontail followed by four of the smallest, fluffiest, cutest baby cottontail rabbits I had ever seen. "Oh, Grandpa, *look*! They're so tiny. They're so *cute*! I just love 'em."

Grandpa just groaned: "I *thought* the corn and lettuce nearest the brush were a little shorter than the rest—now I know why." The cottontails had stopped and were now eating the soft green shoots. I kept whispering, "They're so *cute*, Grandpa. I just love 'em." But I could tell Grandpa didn't love them nearly as much as I did.

Then Grandpa

whispered, "Stevie, look what's coming up from the creek!"

"Oh no! It's a snake!" I hated snakes, and this one was the biggest, meanest, nastiest snake I had ever seen. "What's it going to do?" I asked.

"That is a *big* gopher snake," he said. "Let's watch."

"Oh, Grandpa, he's going to eat the babies!" For the snake headed straight for the baby rabbits.

Grandpa said, "Stevie, sometimes this is the way nature works—the snake may be our friend."

"No, Grandpa, he's like Satan—he's terrible! He's not our friend! He's *not* our friend!"

As we watched the snake sneaking up on the babies, Mama cottontail suddenly spotted the intruder. Disregarding the threat to her own life, she leaped high in the air and landed on the snake's malevolent head. Then she thumped him with her hind feet again and again. The surprised snake pulled back, coiled, and gave her his full attention. He struck, grabbed her soft fur in its mouth, wrapped its full body around her, and began squeezing the life out of her.

"Oh, Grandpa! I hate that snake!"

They were now on the sloping part of the garden. The coiled mass of snake and rabbit started to roll down the hill, *bump, bumpity-bumpity-bump, splash*—right into the creek. The water was so cold, the snake let go!

Mama cottontail was wet and weak but hurried up the bank and across the garden to her babies. The babies were bouncing around in a panic, not knowing what to do. She now tried to herd them into the brush, but the big snake gave her no time to save them.

Though mama cottontail was exhausted from the ordeal, she just couldn't let the snake kill her babies—not even if it meant giving up her life. She attacked the snake again and again, from all directions. The snake coiled, hissed, struck, and missed. He coiled again, and struck again—this time he didn't miss; he got a big bite of fur and once more wrapped his coils around her. By this time, I was screaming, "Grandpa, do something! DO SOMETHING, GRANDPA!"

Just then, they started rolling. Down the slope they went, *bumpity-bumpity-bump*—then *splash!* Once again, the snake let go.

Very slowly, mama cottontail crawled up the bank. She was so weak it now seemed to take her forever to get back. Grandpa had gone downstairs. I followed and stood by the lower deck rail so I wouldn't miss a thing. The snake had now decided to eat her instead of the babies. She was so wet and bedraggled, she now looked tiny to me. Though barely ten feet from her babies, the brave mother had no strength to go any farther. She just lay there waiting for the end. The big snake reached her side, coiled, and prepared for the strike that would leave her babies motherless, when, *whack*! Down came Grandpa's big hoe, and off went mister snake's head. Mama cottontail barely moved. The babies were hopping all around, not knowing what to do or where to go. Grandpa picked up the snake with a pitchfork and carried it away to a place where it could be buried.

* * * * *

It took about half an hour before mama cottontail was strong enough to get up and start crawling toward the thicket. By this time, Grandpa and Grandma had both come out on the porch, and we all watched as the heroic little mother led her babies toward the protection of the brush. Soft-hearted Grandma said, "Why, Papa—the poor dear!"

Grandpa sighed, and said, "Well, Stevie, I guess you and I are going to have to clear some more brush—and plant a bigger garden."

* * * * *

BEADED DEATH

Daniel P. Mannix

As monsters go, the Gila monster of America's West is small indeed. Zookeeper Daniel Mannix remembers one memorable encounter with this feared species, whose bite can result in death.
The very last thing he envisioned was to make pets of "Paul" and "Virginia."

* * * * *

From the red-hot sun that was trying its best to cook the twenty-four houses of Tusca, Arizona, to a deeper black than they were—if such a thing were possible—I stepped into the comparative shade of the porch in front of the Hotel Imperial and prayed that Alex would bring back something in the line of a cool drink besides the specimen boxes for which he had gone to Rashley.

Alex and I were camped in a little ravine a few miles from the town and had spent the summer trying to persuade the wild sheep that they wanted to be photographed. We were going home that afternoon, and he had left me alone in camp. But at noon, when the temperature rose to 110 degrees in the shade—of which there wasn't any—I decided to cheat the black flies and die where I could at least get buried, so I went to the Hotel Imperial.

Inside was an ancient bar, chipped and stained with a couple of wooden boxes of "frozen snow," dug out of the cellar where it had been packed during the winter. There were a few tables held up by chairs, and behind the bar lounged an unkempt individual who had shaved the month before. He was drying glasses with a towel that had seen better days. Intending to get a glass of milk and a chocolate sundae, I veered off and had just sat down by a Mexican at one of the cleaner tables when the swinging door shot open and a cowboy rushed in yelling, "Where's that dude?"

I had never been called a dude before, but being in the West, I had a faint suspicion that he was referring to me. My tablemate, the Mexican, pointed me out at once with the hopeful expression of a boy who sees a friend jogging along with a tin can and who knows where there is a dog.

"Are ye a doctor?" yelled the cowboy.

Evidently, he had seen our research apparatus.

"Yes," said I, hoping they liked doctors.

"Well, come on, then. There's a kid been bit by a lizard."

"You mean by a snake," said I.

"Naw, it's a lizard. One of 'em big red 'uns."

"Gila lizards!" cried the bartender. (He pronounced the word "Heela.")

"Yah. It's Mr. Price's boy."

I was considerably more scared now than before, for my knowledge of medicine is limited, and taking a human life into one's hands is a dangerous thing. However, I did know something about the bites of poisonous lizards and snakes, so with the total population of Tusca, I followed the cowboy toward the last house in the village, where we were met by a Chinese cook, who told us that the boy was dead.

I was horrified and amazed. The bite of a Gila monster, the red, beaded lizard of the West that is one of the only two varieties of poisonous lizards known, is seldom, if ever, fatal. What had happened in this case to cause such sudden death?

The bite of the Gila is dangerous, and by no means to be lightly regarded, for the lizard does not, like a snake, strike once and then retreat. It takes a firm grasp with its flat, stubby head and then grinds the sharp teeth back and forth in the flesh until every last drop of venom in the poison sacs has entered the victim. Like a bulldog, once its jaws meet, it will not let go. But the bite, as a rule, is not fatal to human beings. Some scientists have received reports from people who recovered from such bites with no more inconvenience than if nipped by a small dog.

I wandered about in the little crowd that had collected, asking questions. Little by little, I gathered the following: The boy had had a weak heart combined with lung trouble, and it was partly because of his physical condition that his parents had moved to Arizona. Their doctor had recommended a "dry, warm climate," which was certainly a thumbnail description of Tusca. Poor boy. Possibly it was his father's fault, because the man believed that for a boy to be a "regular fellow," it was necessary for him to kill every wild animal he met, as that was what all "real boys" did.

At any rate, after tormenting all the stray cats and dogs he could find in the little town, he had gone off, accompanied by an Indian boy, to spend the day on the hill that overshadowed the town. A good ten miles from home, while climbing among some great slabs of granite the size of cottages, the boys had come upon a giant Gila sunning itself upon the hot rocks. Gilas usually come out only at night, but this one had evidently decided to enjoy the hot sun before having to search for his supper in the heavy mountain dew of the evening.

The Indian lad had passed him with respect and at a distance, but the white boy, using his climbing stick as a club, had tried to beat the lizard with it, and had made the mistake of getting between the Gila and his hole. The lizard slithered off the rock and made a rush for his home, passing between his attacker's feet. The boy, in a wild effort to escape, fell heavily upon the reptile. The bulldog jaws fastened in the bare calf of his leg, penetrating an artery. The Indian fled, and the boy, with the poison seeping into his veins, tried desperately to loosen the grip of his terrible enemy. Failing, he staggered home, bareheaded in the broiling sun, wild with terror, with the Gila still clinging to him. It was not until he had reached the outskirts of the town that the lizard had dropped off. An hour after reaching the house, the boy was dead of heart failure, caused by a combination of the poison and the shock.

No matter how sorry we may be for the boy, I think most of us would agree that the Gila had the right to defend itself. I have often listened with wonder to hunters, who have traveled miles to shoot big game, refer to the poor, persecuted creatures as "savage and bloodthirsty." I once heard an explorer speak reproachfully of a lion that had attacked him after he had shot it several times. He seemed to think it very unsportsmanlike and narrow-minded of the lion.

But the inhabitants of Tusca were not given to philosophizing, and when an "old-timer" with a frazzled white beard suggested an expedition to find the murderous Gila and also to "clean up all the poisonous pests on that there hill," there were shouts of agreement. The town's entire population, including an assortment of dogs, started off for the hill, breathing vengeance on all the Gilas in creation.

But I felt different. Because Gilas could fight for their lives was no reason—to my mind—why they did not deserve them. Running to the Hotel Imperial, I grabbed a box from the rubbish heap that lay behind the building and then returned to where the crowd had been. It was no longer there, but I could hear shouting, and with the box under one arm and perspiration running off in streams, I managed to dogtrot to the hill.

The crowd had gathered in a ring. Pushing through the circle, I saw the orange-mottled form of the Gila. He had been trying to reach his hole when they had cut him off. Turning slowly around with his mouth half open, showing pearl-white teeth, and making short rushes at his enemies, he was prepared to fight to the death. Death was all he could expect, for his defiant attitude was not one to encourage sympathy.

"Get a gun!" several shouted, and one man tried to hit the Gila with a whip. I popped the box over the lizard and began to speak in what I hoped was a convincing and authoritative tone.

"You've got to drown Gilas," I said. "Don't you know that it's practically impossible to kill them any other way?" That was a lie so terrible that it would have caused my zoology professor to expire could he have heard it.

"Throw it in the Snake," cried someone. The Snake is the little river that runs by Tusca.

Fortunately, the box had a lid, and after a little jiggling with a stick, the Gila was pushed in and the lid popped on. By unanimous consent, I was given the honor of carrying it, and the procession started off with the Gila and me in the lead, and a couple of Mexicans in attendance who kept saying that the poison would leak through the box and kill me. We were halted by a shout, and a scouting party that had gone up the hill ran up to us. One of the men was carrying a Gila tied in an old bit of sacking. As it appeared to be on the point of breaking loose at any moment, we stopped and dumped it into the box with the other, sacking and all.

Our procession reached the Imperial, a hundred yards away from the Snake River. I was about to suggest that we keep the Gilas in a cage for a few days to postpone their death when the hot air was cut by the whistle of the daily train. My followers wavered, and then, mainly from force of habit, ran over to the tracks—there was no station.

Now was my chance. I was standing by the open window of the hotel's storeroom. I hoisted up the box, resting it on the window ledge. I looked cautiously around. The train was stopping with a screaming and howling of brakes and whistle, punctuated by the throbbing, chugging beat of the pistons. No one was watching me. With a short prayer, I shut my eyes and pushed the box into the storeroom. To me it seemed to fall with a crash that shook the building. The rubbish pile was only a few feet away. I grabbed up another box, thanking my stars that they were all of the same make, and sat down on it. Still no one paid any attention to me, and I managed to drop in a large stone and fasten the lid on before the crowd began to form again.

Alex had been on the train, and he now appeared wearing his "city clothes" and a wilted collar. When matters were explained, he instantly said cheerfully, "Open the box and let's see them." There are times when I wonder why someone hasn't shot Alex years ago.

"Can't take any chances of their jumping out," I said, "and furthermore, be quiet!"

He started to object, but something in my eyes silenced him—to my great relief, for the prospect of that tough-looking crowd finding out that I had put the lizards in the local storeroom was distinctly unpleasant.

As we started for the river, Alex suggested that they allow us to take the lizards away when we left the next day. This idea was howled down so angrily that, for the first time since I had been in Tusca, I felt cold, especially about the feet. There is only one thing that you can be sure of with Alex—that he will always say the wrong thing—so I decided not to prolong matters. The crowd began to suspect that all was not well, and several voices called out to me to throw the box far out in the stream; the men thought that I might try to let the lizards slip out at the last moment. To throw that box as far as possible was just what I had every intention of doing. It lit almost in midstream and was rushed away by the swift current. The stone had been heavy, and the box sank fast, whirling and dancing lower and lower in the water until it disappeared in the crest of the rapids below the town.

The crowd slowly broke up, and after I had told Alex where the Gilas were and what he was, we slipped off to the storeroom and got in by a door that creaked loudly enough to be heard a mile away. One Gila was out trying to bury himself in an open crate of granulated sugar. The other had become tangled in the bag and was struggling to get loose. Alex suggested naming one "Virginia." He had a girl with red hair named Virginia, and so, of course, the other certainly had to be "Paul."

I approached Paul, and he left the sugar and stood on guard. I took another step, and he leaped forward with his stumpy legs rigid. Raising his head, he let forth a curiously hair-raising hissing sound. Having given his warning, he looked up at me with his mouth half open as if he were grinning.

I had intended to pick him up by his thick tail, but—well, why hurt the poor thing? I used a shovel to scoop him up and replace him and his wife in the box. (At the time, we had no way of telling whether or not they were a pair, but as it proved later, they were.)

We kept the Gilas at the camp for the rest of the day and for the whole of that night. We were kept busy packing and labeling specimen cases, and when our boxes were loaded on the backs of pack-mules the next morning, I was carrying a suitcase in the lid of which several holes had been carefully and inconspicuously punched.

The baggage was unloaded from the pack-mules, the train came whistling and panting in from the burning desert, and our boxes and trunks were slung aboard. The conductor came up to speak to us, checking over a long roll of tickets and baggage receipts.

"You aren't taking anything alive, are you?" he asked.

"I suppose dogs and cats have to ride in the baggage car?" I replied, not particularly eager to answer directly.

"Yes, but it's things like white rats or chipmunks we're after."

"Oh, no," I said. "We don't have anything of *that* sort." And we didn't. No one could call Gila monsters either white rats or chipmunks.

Paul and Virginia had grown restless during this conversation and had begun to stamp about on the hard leather bottom of the suitcase. I put the suitcase down quickly and talked as loudly as possible until the conductor moved away. Several people had begun to gather about me, and looking down, I saw to my horror that the suitcase was swaying like a reed in a storm. The crowd was eyeing it rather curiously, and I felt that it was time to grab the suitcase and jump aboard. Through the window I could see that several people were having an argument and that the crowd was growing. After what seemed several hundred years, the sweet sound of the double "toot" sounded, and the train slowly began to move away.

During the long trip east, we occasionally gave the Gilas water from the little pasteboard cups, holding the cups in our hands for a while to take the chill off of the ice water. They drank but would not eat much.

At Philadelphia we were met by our ancient station wagon which we loaded with our luggage. Then we set out for home. At the end of the long four-hour trip in the country, Alex was dropped off at his home with a promise to come over the next day and see Paul and Virginia in their new quarters. I arrived home to find my family in the death throes of giving a dance.

Everyone greeted me effusively and set me to moving furniture. Father and the gardener were rolling up the rugs and putting them where the guests wouldn't fall over them as they came in. My sister's beau was shoving a table about in an aimless sort of way. The only people who were having a good time were two little kids who had been called in to slide up and down on the newly waxed floor to make it slippery smooth.

I very cautiously slipped out to the flower conservatory on the porch and put the Gilas in a big cage with glass sides and a wire top that held the horned toads and the desert swifts in winter. I was a little worried at their appearance. Their flat, heavy tails had shrunk and were thin and flabby. Like camels' humps, these tails serve as food reserves for the lizards, and during the long train ride, they had lived on the food stored away there. I gave them some water and they began to move slowly about, investigating their new home, stretching along the floor, touching the sides and sand bottom with their delicate, flickering, snakelike tongues.

There had been no casualties in my zoo during my absence. On the contrary, there were eight new baby skunks who stamped and growled at me and watched with amazement while their parents came up to have their heads scratched. The raccoons and opossums were off for the day on business of their own in the woods. Captain Flint, the parrot, whistled and shrieked with delight and spent the rest of the day riding about on my shoulder, his first vacation from his cage since I had left. Rags' greeting showed me once again that the best pet in the world is a dog. It was a successful homecoming, and I did not visit the Gilas again until after dark.

The orchestra had arrived and everyone was doing some last-minute dressing when I sneaked out to the conservatory, in bare feet and khaki trousers, to give Paul and Virginia their first fresh eggs. There was no light in the conservatory, so I took a box of matches with me. Once inside, I closed the door carefully and struck a match.

The glass cage was empty! The match flickered out, and I quickly struck another. Yes, they were gone—but how? There was no way they could have escaped. As I examined the cage, I noticed that one pane of glass looked strangely clear. I reached out and put my hand through it. The frame was empty.

The second match went out, and in groping about for the matchbox, which I had put on the top of an iron plant table, I managed to push it off onto the floor. The floor was damp, and as I bent over to feel for the box, I heard the sound of one of the Gilas slithering slowly and splashily upon the wet boards.

The dark is ordinarily unpleasant of itself, and in that conservatory it was pitch-black. I suddenly remembered that one of these Gilas had killed a human being . . . and that I was barefoot. I heard the swishing sound again. It seemed to come from all sides. Was I hearing only one, or both? If one, where was the other? I tried to feel for the matchbox again, but to run my hand over the floor took more courage than I had. I made another feel for the matches and touched something hard and beady. Then I stood still and let the sweat run off while I yelled for help.

I had been mentally bitten a dozen or more times before I heard my sister come singing down the hall. She opened the door and peered into the darkness.

"Who's here?" she said.

"Sis," said I, "have you your shoes on?"

"Of course, I have satin pumps on. Why?"

"Will you come in and hand me the matches that are over by the door?" said I, knowing that a box is always kept there.

"Why on earth couldn't you get them yourself?" I heard the matches being found and then the clacking of French heels across the floor. "Here they are."

I groped for her hand, got the matches, lit one, and looked around. The coast was clear. The hordes of Gila monsters that had been biting me had vanished.

While the match still burned, I made a dash for the door, staggered through it, and lit the light in the hall. Then I sat down and panted.

"Are you crazy?" asked my sister.

"No," I said, wiping my forehead, "but those two Gilas are loose on the floor somewhere and—"

I did not have to finish. French heels or no French heels, she got across that slippery floor in record time, and Paul and Virginia had the conservatory to themselves.

"Good heavens, they can't get into the house, can they?" she panted.

Just then came a shriek from the living room where one of the maids was dusting.

"Yes," I said gravely, "they can."

We rushed into the living room. The maid had collapsed into the arms of the leader of the orchestra, who seemed considerably puzzled. Her dust brush lay halfway beneath a bookcase, and after a little effort I pulled it out, disclosing Virginia, who had taken a firm grip on the bristles. I knew better than to try prying her loose, so I carried brush and Gila off to my own private greenhouse. Then I put the tree-frogs in the chameleon's cage and gave Virginia their old home temporarily.

I returned to the house to find the leader describing to the rest of the orchestra something between a brontosaurus and a boa constrictor. They were all greatly interested to hear that there was another one loose and climbed rather hurriedly upon the platform built for them at the far corner of the room.

The afternoon's excitement was nothing to what went on during the hour before the guests began to arrive. My sister swore with tears in her eyes that she would not give a dance with a poisonous lizard loose in the house. Mother suggested that as cobras are fond of music—at least you always see snake-charmers blowing on pipes—the Gila would be, too, and the orchestra ought to play and lure him out. Father thought this a charming idea, and as we did not know from what room Paul was in, he suggested that the musicians parade through the house, playing gentle melodies as they went. This they indignantly refused to do, saying that they had been hired as a dance orchestra, not as lizard serenaders.

It was impossible to keep the guests from knowing, as some of the early arrivals had helped in the search. Unfortunately, Jessie, my pet crow, who has a passion for sneaking out from behind chairs and nipping girls on the ankles, turned up and several times caused a near riot. But at last the dance was over, and while we were eating the remains of the buffet supper and holding a post-mortem generally, we heard *thump!* . . . *thump!* . . . *thump!* coming from the floor as if someone were walking upside down on the ceiling of the room below.

"It's Paul!" I cried, jumping up. "He's underneath the floorboards!"

"If it is, he must be wearing hip boots to make all that racket," said my father skeptically.

It was Paul. I pried up a few boards and poked about with a broom. It was too dark to see anything, so I pulled the broom up and went for a flashlight. The flashlights in our house have a strange ability to disappear when wanted, and while I was burrowing in a closet, I heard a wild scream from the kitchen. That long-suffering maid who had already met Virginia that evening, being a tidy person, had carried the broom back to the kitchen and had found Paul clinging to the end. He must have seized the broom while I was poking it beneath the floor and been brought up from the depths unnoticed. As an experiment, I hung the broom up over the cage where his wife was and waited to see how long he would hold on. It was an hour before his jaws finally loosened their grip and he slipped off.

* * * * *

During the winter, Paul and Virginia grew very tame. They ate raw eggs almost exclusively, and it was an interesting sight to see them lapping up the golden yolk with their forked tongues.

I made them a cactus-garden home with hot pipes running through the sand to keep it dry. The cacti were in pots sunk into the sand so that they could be watered without wetting the whole enclosure. The walls of their apartment were of smooth cement, and as the Gilas could not climb, I did not bother to cover it.

There is only one person allowed in my greenhouse. That is the six-year-old daughter of our next-door neighbor. She is the only person I have ever met who is more fond of animals than I am, and as she has learned not to touch the delicate plants or disturb the aquariums and always to shut the door after her, she has a free run of the little glass-covered garden. One day in early March, I saw Betty going toward the greenhouse with a toothbrush. That afternoon, while my family and I were calling next door, I asked her mother what Betty had been doing with the brush.

The mother gave me a curious look and left the room. We could hear her calling Betty, and after a few minutes we heard Betty answer.

There followed a half-audible conversation, ending with a cry of horror, and the woman appeared, dragging Betty by the hand.

"She says she's been using it to scratch the backs of those lizards of yours, and it was *my* toothbrush! What on earth should I do?"

I assured her that there was no chance of the brush being poisoned, and all seemed well until Betty was told not to play with the Gilas. The poor child raised a wail to high heaven, and at last a compromise was reached whereby she was provided with a special toothbrush on the end of a stick for scratching purposes! In return she promised not to dress the Gilas up in doll clothes and not to play with them.

Under Betty's careful tutelage, I began to handle the Gilas, rather gingerly at first, but as they showed unmistakable pleasure at having their backs and stomachs rubbed, I slowly became convinced that they were completely friendly and tame.

In June a leak developed in the wooden tank over their home, and some water trickled in a corner of the cactus garden. I found Virginia working in the damp sand and tried to move her, but for the first time she hissed and snapped at me. I let her alone, and the next morning she had moved away again.

Damp sand is likely to give most desert reptiles stomach cramps, so I began to dig it out—and found a clutch of leathery white eggs. Virginia was a mother. I hurriedly buried them again, and feeling sure that Virginia knew better than I what they needed to hatch, I kept the sand damp. A month later the little Gilas hatched—tiny creatures, brilliantly colored.

Even I realized that it would be impossible to keep fourteen Gila monsters, so I passed them on to Mr. John MacNamee, who is working his way through college by "milking" poisonous reptiles. The antitoxin used for snake bites comes from the venom of the snake itself, and MacNamee raises poisonous snakes and "milks" them of their venom by a painless process. The venom he sells to hospitals.

Paul and Virginia are now in the Philadelphia Zoo, where more people have a chance to admire them, and where they are the pride and joy of Mr. Brown, the curator of reptiles at the zoo.

I think the Gilas are happy. They are all quite tame and even submit to the indignity of being "milked" without protest. Poor Paul! To think that because he defended himself against the cruel boy, unthinking people would have condemned him to a horrible death! I do not believe that he misses the desert; with a large run, a special diet, and a loving wife and family, he is no doubt contented to be where he is. If he took one human life, he has saved five others by his poison in antitoxin form, and may save many more. Treated kindly, he and his wife have become interesting and friendly pets, showing that even the "red death of the western deserts" is not as red as he is painted.

* * * * *

"Beaded Death," by Daniel P. Mannix. Published in St. Nicholas, *February 1934. Original text owned by Joe Wheeler. Daniel P. Mannix of Philadelphia was well known during the first half of the twentieth century as the Keeper of the Back-Yard Zoo. His true-life animal stories were carried by popular magazines of his day.*

A LOVE THAT KEPT HIM WARM

Penny Porter

Why on earth had the tiny hummingbird (weighing less than two-tenths of an ounce) forgotten to fly south?
Was he hurt?

* * * * *

One chill December morning, my husband, Bill, and I spotted a tiny hummingbird warming his tummy feathers in front of a spotlight attached to our cattle ranch's desert-based windmill. "Poor little thing," I murmured. "It looks like he forgot to fly south."

"Forgot?" Bill frowned. "Birds don't forget."

"Then he's hurt?" I said. *Surely he will die.*

Hummingbirds always left our Arizona cattle ranch in mid-September to migrate more than two thousand miles into the tropical jungles of Central America. There they would be safe from the freezing winds that swept up from the Gulf of Mexico into the desert lands of Cochise County in the great Southwest. But why, this year, did one tiny, jewel-like bird stay behind? How could he possibly survive?

This was a Costa's hummingbird, among the smallest of the species. Although he would weigh less than two-tenths of an ounce on a scale, he had to eat insects and nectar every minute to replace the calories he burned. But this was winter, and now he was alone in a corner of the world where temperatures could fluctuate sixty-five to seventy-five degrees in less than twenty-four hours. Nothing was left to keep him alive, and nothing to keep him warm—except the shelter he sought in the nearby adobe hut and a lightbulb.

On this particular morning, the mesquite, manzanita, and prairie grasses crackled and snapped in the frigid air. We did the only thing we could. We hung a feeder of sugar water close to the warm spotlight to keep the liquid from freezing. As we wired the glass container to the windmill, the little bird buzzed beelike around our heads. "He seems to know we're trying to help," I said. *But will sugar water alone be enough to sustain him?*

Perhaps it was, because when spring came, our hummingbird was not only still alive, but his colors seemed brighter as he darted among banks of budding wild roses and zoomed across fields of lavender alfalfa. We liked to think his second chance at life was due to our helping hands. But over the next twelve years, we learned his survival was part of something far greater—the most powerful link to life in the Master's plan—love.

As days grew warmer, we watched this busy, living gem sip nectar from flowers, catch gnats in midair with his tongue, and skewer moths and wasps with his needle-nosed bill, and it wasn't long before we realized that most of his daylight hours were spent defending his territory against the return of the enemy. Like a miniature gun ship, he bent his tail in rudderlike fashion and flew backward and forward and upside down. Chattering angrily, he attacked woodpeckers and doves, and chased away birds *ten times* his size. He fought relentlessly, even against his own kind, for what he seemed to feel was his.

"Wow! He's a humdinger," Bill said one day. "That'd be a good name for a little creature who's always at war with the world."

I agreed. But there had to be a reason for battle, a purpose to his territorial behavior. Only when evenings came did the whirring wings give way to quieter moments, and we'd see the little bird perched on the rotating windmill rudder. Facing the south, he waited.

Love arrived in April—a drab little hummingbird in shades of dusty gray. From his lofty roost, Humdinger watched this tiny shadow of his own radiance build her walnut-sized nest on a forgotten lasso looped over a nearby fence. He forgot about war. Instead, he took up sky dancing, tracing intricate patterns against fiery sunsets as love crept into his heart.

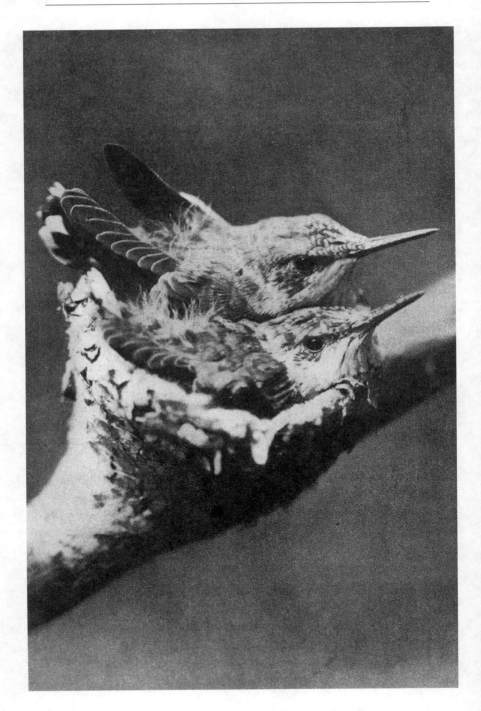

Soon, the tiny female joined him, and a mating ritual followed. Scolding and squeaking in morning's splendor, they showered in misty rainbows cast by pasture sprinklers. They preened and puffed amid dawn-lit spiderwebs and played hide-and-seek among snowy yucca bells. At last, exhibiting his feathers in their most vibrant, jewel-like colors—ruby, emerald, and amethyst— Humdinger wooed and won his tiny Cinderella in a graceful nuptial dive.

Two white, pea-size eggs appeared in the nest. Two tiny babies hatched and were fed and nurtured by two parents who loved them. Not until they were mature enough to tackle life on their own did they finally fly away. After that, it wasn't unusual to see the evening silhouettes of Humdinger and Cinderella, two of earth's tiniest creatures, perched side by side on the tail of the windmill rudder. Then, September came. And Cinderella flew away.

Why didn't he go with her? I wondered anew. Unable to accept that I was witnessing one of nature's great mysteries, I continued to think something was wrong with him, or that Cinderella had simply tired of him. Could he survive another winter alone?

I needn't have worried. Humdinger did survive, and year after year when spring returned, Cinderella brought love to his life again. Wars were forgotten in lieu of sky dancing, taking showers, making love, and raising babies. And every autumn, when the September nights dipped and winter snarled down from the mountains, she left him.

For twelve years, Humdinger never left the ranch. We replaced the lightbulb each November. In March the wars began. And since wildlife patterns and habits are changeless, twilight found our little hummingbird sitting alone on the windmill rudder, facing south—waiting—waiting for Cinderella to return.

His thirteenth winter came. *Will he still be there?* I wondered as I filled the hummingbird feeder with sugar water and took it with me, for I am a creature of hope. There was a cold snap in the air that night. Bill turned up his sheepskin-lined collar. "Maybe I'll go with you," he said. Heading toward the pasture, the walk seemed farther than it used to. I thought about other years, when the tiny bird would see us coming, his brilliant jewel-flashes glinting in the night with colors that appear only in dreams. But this night seemed too quiet. I braced myself for disappointment, moved closer, and hung the feeder at the bottom of the windmill. A calf bawled in the darkness, and an owl hooted its warning. No Humdinger. We turned to head home.

That's when I heard a whirring of wings, and there, warming his tummy feathers against the spotlight, hovered a shabby little hummingbird. Gone were the flashing colors of youth, but he was surviving, waiting for love, just like we all do. Then, when April comes, I mused, with luck he'll still be around to remind us . . . it takes more than a lightbulb . . . *It's love that keeps us warm.*

* * * * *

"A Love That Kept Him Warm," by Penny Porter. Published in Penny Porter's Adobe Secrets. *Copyright © 2006. Reprinted by permission of the author. More of Penny Porter's true-life animal stories have been published by* Reader's Digest *than those of any other author. Today, she lives and writes from her home in Tucson, Arizona.*

CHATTER, THE STOWAWAY CHIPMUNK

Dee Dunsing

Stacy Brock was determined to impress her citified Uncle Felix with her own sophistication—but alas! To meet him a soggy wreck on a chicken-coop raft with Chatter (her pet chipmunk on her shoulder), how much more humiliating could it get!

* * * * *

Stacy Brock adjusted her collar of her gray-and-white linen dress, smoothed back her curling hair, and tried not to notice how the imperfect mirror distorted her pink-cheeked face. This was the best mirror in the ranch house—in fact, the only one—and to Stacy, who had never known the smooth quicksilver reflections of a better mirror, it seemed quite all right.

As she turned toward her cot to pick up the new white mail-order hat, she gave a little shriek and then a lusty command: "Chatter! Get away from there!"

A tame chipmunk, which had been about to curl up on the hat in a ray of sunlight, darted back and ran like a lightning streak up the curtain.

With a sigh of relief, Stacy picked up the hat, gingerly put it on, and looked at herself again. She was trying to look like her cousin, Rhoda Graves, whose golden-haired loveliness had so impressed everyone during her visit

two years ago. Rhoda had worn a gray-and-white linen dress then, and a white hat. She had seemed exquisitely dainty and poised and aloof, something that Stacy was afraid her own brown-skinned sturdiness would never achieve.

But if she could just look and act almost the same as Rhoda, Stacy had thought, Uncle Felix would like her—and maybe Aunt Jane and Rhoda would too. At least the idea had relieved the terrible panicky feeling that almost swamped Stacy when she learned that she was going to live with her professor uncle and his family in their home in the East. Uncle Felix wouldn't want a barbarian in his house, she knew. But if she could manage to look and act just a little bit like Rhoda, she would belong there, would fit in. Then Uncle Felix wouldn't feel ashamed of his western ward and niece.

Stacy gave a little shriek again as she saw Chatter coming down the curtain. "Get away!" she ordered. "I like you, but you simply mustn't get up on my shoulder and knock this hat off!"

And at Chatter's hurt retirement, she opened her dresser drawer, got out a piñon nut, and threw it to him.

"I didn't mean to hurt your feelings, Chatter," Stacy apologized. "It's just that overalls and an old straw hat are different from city clothes. You may knock my straw hat off any time, Chatter. You know that. In fact, I like to have you knock it off because it's your way of saying you love me."

Then, as she remembered that she would not be wearing overalls and an old straw hat again and that in half an hour she would be saying goodbye to Chatter, Stacy picked up her white shoes and began furiously dabbing white cleaner over a microscopic spot.

"I—I'll have you up to visit me, Chatter," she promised in a tear-choked voice. "I'll find somebody who's coming up that way real soon, Chatter. When the floods stop, people'll start traveling around again; and I'll manage to get you even if I have to ride a hundred miles or so."

Chatter wasn't paying a lot of attention. He didn't recognize shades of emotion, particularly those of the human type. And the prospect of Stacy's leaving him was such a new experience that he couldn't have imagined it even if he had understood her words. He went on busily eating his piñon nut there on the windowsill, grinding away with his sharp little teeth, picking out the sweet nut meat. When he had finished, he stood erect and rubbed both paws gently up and down his tan-furred stomach as if to say that this piñon nut was the most delicious one he had ever tasted.

* * * * *

The ranch house, nestling in its grove of cottonwoods, was almost hidden by sage hills as Stacy looked back. After her goodbye to Chatter and the ranch folks, she had kept her eyes on the red dirt road and tried not to let her emotions run away with her. It wasn't in the western tradition for people to cry, no matter how much they felt like it; and Stacy had been raised in that tradition. Besides, crying would muss her all up; and she was meeting Uncle Felix down at Blue Cañon and wanted most awfully to look cool and beautiful and self-contained, like Rhoda.

When at last Stacy did glance back over the sputtering exhaust pipe of the old car, she made a quick about-face, blew her nose violently, and pushed the gas choke in and out of the dashboard till the motor bucked like a steer and almost died.

It was well that she heard the funny noise in the car within the next mile or two. It took her attention, helped her forget that she was leaving all her old friends and going into a strange new world where the people were awfully stiff and probably wouldn't like her. She noticed the sound first because it resembled Chatter's little squeak when he was in trouble. It seemed to come from somewhere around the rear of the car, near the rear wheels.

At first she leaned out and listened to it, but she could tell nothing. Then, fearing that maybe a wheel might come off, she stopped the car and got out. No sign of anything wrong.

Stacy got back in and drove for a mile or two. The noise was baffling. Sometimes it sounded on the bumpy parts of the road and sometimes on the smooth ones. It was like nothing that Stacy had ever heard in all her three years of running the automobile.

Then suddenly it stopped. She didn't hear it again until she got to the creek road.

The rivers of the Southwest—always high at springtime—had flooded their banks this year and washed out bridges, levees, and whole farms. Even Chokecherry Creek—a small mountain stream normally—was nearly fifty feet across, roaring like a full-sized river. In Red Rock Valley, it had washed over the road that Stacy was following.

She stopped the car, debated a moment whether or not she could cross the overflow. Then she thought of Uncle Felix waiting at Blue Cañon and realized that she must get there on time.

Driving slowly, Stacy started across. The water rose around the tires of the car, rose till it covered the hubcaps.

Suddenly a faint splash and frantic squeaks drew her attention. Turning, she saw Chatter trying desperately to swim toward the car but being drawn out by the clashing currents of the flood-swollen stream.

Too surprised to speak, she stepped hard on the gas pedal and spun through the water toward dry land. Hardly waiting for the car to stop, she hopped out and ran toward the water's edge. Chatter had been sucked into the tumultuous creek until now he was almost a quarter of the way across.

She gave only an instant's thought to her clothes. She had to get in there and save Chatter, or he would drown. He had followed her, stowed away somewhere in the back part of the car—faithful little creature—and been caught in the water when she drove through it. She couldn't desert him now.

With a run she was in the icy river. Soon she was swimming with all her hard-muscled strength. Chatter tried to swim to her, but he was a helpless speck in a whirl of foam. He dodged a cottonwood branch, looked pleadingly at Stacy as if to say, "I can't hold out much longer. When are you going to help me?"

Stacy herself was having trouble with the swift current. If she could only put her head down and do a quick crawl for a minute, she thought she could reach Chatter. But she still had that new white hat on, and a crawl stroke would float it off. She wanted to preserve something of that beautiful ensemble she had put on so proudly this morning for the benefit of Uncle Felix. So she dug her arms fiercely into the water and pulled close to Chatter.

At last she could reach him. She seized his little wet body in one fist and set him on her shoulder where he clung, shivering pathetically. Now if she could only get back to shore—

But Stacy had reckoned without the spring turbulence of Chokecherry. Already she had been swept a fifth of a mile beyond the car and well out into the middle of the stream. She tried swimming toward shore, but discovered suddenly that she was awfully cold and tired, that she couldn't make it.

Maybe one of those logs—or tree branches—would keep her afloat till she could get her breath. She glanced wildly around. There were no logs.

But close at hand, so close that a stroke or two would take her to it, was an empty chicken coop—a crude homemade thing fashioned from small logs—a ridiculous but stout refuge.

Stacy struck out for it, reached it, and hung on it thankfully. At least she and Chatter were both alive. When she got her breath she would swim in to shore.

And her hat—at least she still had that. Only the edges of it were a little wet. She could still meet Uncle Felix in a decent hat.

* * * * *

The sun had dipped behind Bald Mountain. The whirling, eddying creek roared its triumph to the deepening dusk. Two miles upstream around a palisade of dark rock lay Blue Cañon, its lights shining like beacons.

Stacy, atop her chicken coop in the middle of the river, eyed the lights uncertainly. She would never have chosen this way to enter Blue Cañon to meet Uncle Felix. Never! Her gray-and-white dress, dry now after the long ride in the sun, was a mass of wrinkles. Her white shoes were stained, soggy things. And her hat—well, Chatter had climbed on her shoulder one time during the afternoon when she was not on guard and had knocked it off. She had watched it float downstream, preceding her for almost a mile before it sank.

Her original plan for swimming to shore had come to nothing, because by the time she had got her breath back the car was miles behind, Chatter was shivering as if he were going to die, and she herself felt loath to get back into the icy water. Besides, she knew that if she once got off that chicken coop and failed to get to shore, she'd never get back on it again.

So Stacy sat very still, clinging to the coop, and watched Blue Cañon come closer, while a sun-dried and frisky Chatter explored all the possible climbing places on their raft.

When she got very near Blue Cañon, she saw that the river came almost up to the bridge. She could easily get onto it from her barge, probably without getting wet again.

There were people on the bridge too. A dozen or more of them. With a rush of color to her face, Stacy realized that they had sighted the strange party on the coop and had gathered there to help her off. By straining her eyes, she made out someone whom she thought to be Uncle Felix. Yes, it was Uncle Felix—in a white linen suit, with Panama hat and cane. Faultlessly dressed and neat as always, while she—she rode into Blue Cañon on a chicken coop, her clothes mangled, hatless, and a pet chipmunk in the crook of one arm!

Stacy felt terrible to think that she had bungled everything. Now her future life—her life with Uncle Felix and Aunt Jane and Rhoda—would start wrong. They would think of her as a crude, rough, primitive type who could never change, who would humiliate them in their home by her lack of grace. They wouldn't like her, she knew. No family which kept itself as faultlessly attired, as perfectly poised as they did, would like a barbarian in their midst.

The bridge was looming up before her. She would have to stand up, grasp it, and jump over its rail. She seized Chatter, and tossed him forward toward a dozen waiting hands. Then she herself was at the bridge, and the same hands willingly reached out to help her.

* * * * *

"Uncle Felix, I—I'm sorry about having Chatter with me," Stacy apologized to a grave-faced gentleman, as the two of them rode in her uncle's car up toward the Hotel Nancy. "I'll leave him here in town, and somebody from the ranch can get him later on."

Uncle Felix looked at her with mild surprise. "Don't you want to take him with you?"

Stacy stared at him as if he had spoken sacrilege. "I—I couldn't take him with me, could I, Uncle—not to your home and Aunt Jane's?"

"And what's the matter with my home?" Uncle Felix questioned. "Isn't it good enough for him?"

Stacy could hardly believe her ears. "Why—why," she stammered, not knowing what to say, "it—of course it's good enough for him. It— it's too good, I guess. That's what I meant."

"Absurd," reassured her uncle.

Stacy caught her breath, unable to believe the good news. Was that a twinkle in Uncle Felix's eye? She ventured an experimental question: "What kind of girls do you like, Uncle Felix, besides ones that have gray-and-white dresses and are graceful and poised?"

Uncle Felix chuckled. "That sounds like Rhoda," he remarked. Then more thoughtfully, "I do consider that she has achieved a certain distinction in her dress and bearing. But if anyone else—" he held up a hand in warning, "if anyone else did the same things, that person would be an imitator. And I like individuals, not imitators."

"Oh," said Stacy softly. She smoothed back her bedraggled hair and surveyed her muscular brown arm. Then, "What would you think of a girl who got all dressed up to come into town to meet a dignified uncle, and then jumped into a creek to save a pet chipmunk, and arrived floating down the river on top of a chicken coop?"

"I should say she was a first-rate individualist," replied Uncle Felix, with emphasis. "I should say I would be proud to have her as a member of my family—and likewise the chipmunk."

Stacy felt a sudden desire to embrace Uncle Felix, to sob on his immaculate shoulder and tell him about all the doubts she had felt concerning her guardian and her new home. But those things would not be altogether pleasant for Uncle Felix to hear; and besides, it was not in the western tradition to sob. So she sat up very straight, blinked her tear-moist eyes, and grinned happily.

And Chatter—whose distinction between persons was very subtle, and between clothes very unsubtle—jumped suddenly to Uncle Felix's shoulder, where he knocked off that gentleman's spotless white Panama hat.

* * * * *

"Chatter, the Stowaway Chipmunk" [originally "Stacy Dresses Up"], by Dee Dunsing. Published in The Girl's Companion, June 7, 1936. Text printed by permission of Joe Wheeler (P.O. Box 1246, Conifer, CO 80433) and David C. Cook, Colorado Springs, Colorado. Dee Dunsing wrote for popular magazines during the first half of the twentieth century.

A Bug Tale

Mary Perrine

"Doodlebug, doodlebug, come out of your hole. Doodlebug, doodlebug, come out of your hole, doodlebug—"
Grandpa was not amused—so he decided to stop the racket.

* * * * *

"Doodlebug, doodlebug, come out of your hole. Doodlebug, doodlebug, come out of your hole, doodlebug—"

Grandfather Lane stirred uneasily in his sleep. The voice once again broke the stillness. "Doodlebug, doodlebug, come out of your hole."

This time Grandfather pushed himself into a sitting position. There was an irritated look on his face.

Oh, yes, he was used to all city noises. But how anyone could grow accustomed to this country racket was beyond him. Two days ago he had arrived at son Jake's house, and in this short time his nerves were constantly on edge. He marveled that his city-reared son could love the country so completely.

Now with that hair-raising noise blurring his mind, he could only decide something must be done, and done soon.

So Grandfather pulled on his new boots and stalked with a meaningful gait in the direction of the racket.

Just around the old-fashioned well house he came full upon the culprit. Of all things! It was his granddaughter.

"Kate!" he exclaimed, as he pulled his whiskers and blinked in wonder.

"*Shh!*" with emphasis. This came from the girl, who was bending low to the ground. Her indignant glance told him plainly that he was an intruder.

Then again, "Doodlebug, doodlebug, come out of your hole."

This brought Grandfather to his senses. He took another step. "Kate," he commanded in a tone none too soft. "Look here, can't you stop that noise? You aren't practicing for a program, are you?"

Kate settled back reluctantly. "Oh Gramps," she sighed, "I give up. Can't you let me get my doodlebugs?"

The very idea sent shivers down the old man's back. He groped for a question. "What *are* doodlebugs, anyway?"

The eleven-year-old pushed a brown pigtail over one shoulder with a grimy hand, then handed a shallow pan of sandy dirt to her grandfather.

He took it gingerly. Kate stood up. She poked in the dirt with her finger. Something gray stirred and strove to wriggle out of sight.

"There are four doodlebugs in there," she announced, "and if you hadn't come I would have five by now."

"What are they *for?*" asked Grandfather in his please-forgive-me voice. "Just a nasty little bug."

"Huh," scoffed Kate, "show me another bug that hides in funny little holes and will come if you call it long enough."

"Indeed," said Grandpa. "Is that right? What do doodlebugs eat?"

"Why, I don't know," Kate admitted. "They never said." She giggled and finished, "Dirt, maybe."

"Well, there is one way to find out." He grasped Kate's arm, saying, "Let's go see the encyclopedia." His thought was, *Anything to get her away from here.*

As soon as the porch was under his feet, Grandpa made a beeline for the swing, and, settling comfortably, he directed, "Now, Katie, wash your hands, find the right volume, and read about your bug."

The girl disappeared.

When she returned with the book, she saw that she was not a minute too soon. Grandpa's eyes were closing for a delayed nap.

He roused himself and murmured, "What does it say, Katie?"

She leafed through the book, then announced, "It says, 'See ant lion.' "

"Ant lion," repeated Grandfather. "Well, go find the A-N-T volume."

That was easy and soon Kate was back, searching for the right page.

"Here it is," she declared, then began to read in her clear young style. "The ant lion is an insect that digs a pit in the soil, in which it traps ants and other small insects for its food."

"All right," said Grandpa, "that's enough. It eats ants, as one would judge from its name."

Kate was not listening. A moment later she broke out, "Oh, listen, Gramps. It describes the doodlebug. It says that on its head it has a pair of jaws like long sharp swords, and three pairs of legs are fastened close behind its head, so that it has to walk backward all the time."

"Three pairs!" exclaimed her grandfather. "That's enough to make anyone walk backward."

Kate began to read again. "The ant lion usually chooses a place with dry, sandy soil for its pit. It starts work by walking around and around backward, pushing its tail like a shovel down into the sand behind it. The sand slides over its back and head. By jerking suddenly from time to time, it throws the sand to one side. It moves in a smaller and smaller circle, continuing to dig. When it reaches the center, it has formed a funnel-shaped hole in the earth. This, its pit, is sometimes two inches wide and one or more inches deep."

"My," interrupted Grandfather, "you'd think this bug had brain power to do all that, wouldn't you? I suppose it's instinct."

Kate nodded, continuing, "It hides under the sand at the bottom. If an ant crawls near, the loose sand slides under it. The waiting ant lion throws sand to make it fall faster. When it is within reach, he kills it and sucks the juice for food.

"Why, the mean old thing," she cried, looking up from the page indignantly.

"Oh, I don't know," was Grandfather's reply. "I have read about the ant, and if I remember right, they have wars, kill one another, and make slaves of aphids. That is nature, and if Mr. Ant wants to survive, he must beware of loose sand."

"That's right," admitted Kate as she turned back to the book. "When full grown, the ant lion makes a cocoon and rests quietly. When at last it becomes an adult, it has a long body and four transparent wings. There are many species."

Kate stopped. "Why, Grandpa," she exclaimed, "isn't that interesting and strange? Well, that is all there is here about my doodlebugs, except that they form the family of *M-y-r-m-e-l-e-o-n-t-i-d-a-e*," she spelled. "And don't forget they belong to the family order of *N-e-u-r-o-p-t-e-r-a*."

"Good for them." Grandfather smiled.

Kate hurriedly took the book inside. She reappeared almost immediately, and her intentions to leave were obvious.

"Say, young lady," called Grandfather, "where are you going?" Of course, he knew.

She answered, "To get some more doodlebugs."

"Well," he laughed as she ran down the steps, "beware of loose sand!"

* * * * *

"A Bug Tale," by Mary Perrine. Published in The Youth's Instructor, *April 13, 1948. Text printed by permission of Joe Wheeler (P.O. Box 1246, Conifer, CO 80433) and Review and Herald® Publishing Association, Hagerstown, Maryland. Mary Perrine wrote for inspirational magazines around the mid-twentieth century.*

GUINEVERE, THE MOUSE
Daze of Chivalry

B. J. Chute

What possible relationship could a two hundred-pound fullback and a two-ounce mouse have with each other?
Therein hangs this unforgettable story.

* * * * *

"I don't give a darn what you say," said Hugh Nagel. "This team needs just one thing and that one thing is a fullback, and until we get one the whole business is going to be fooey."

"We have a fullback," Tom Martin protested lazily, rolling over on a locker-room bench and nearly falling off. "We have a large, not to say enormous, fullback, and it's a well-known fact that a given team can have only one fullback at a time. That's an old geometric theorem, that is."

"Old geometric theorem your grandmother," said Hugh irritably. "You just won't listen to reason."

"Who's afraid of the big bad fullback?" Captain Gerry Lynn inquired musically.

"That's just it." Hugh launched spiritedly on a one-sided debate. "No one's afraid of him and what good, I ask you, is a perfectly tame fullback? None. And Truck is just as gentle and patient and—dumb—as an elephant.

His idea of playing football is to move around in a sort of daze and apologize when he bumps into anyone and knocks him over. Now I ask you—" He made a sweeping gesture. "I like Truck, he's a good scout—"

"A dumb egg with a yolk of gold," Gerry murmured helpfully.

"Be serious," said Hugh. "I really mean this. It's getting me down."

"I know how you feel," Tom interjected, "but what's to be done about it? It's not as if we had any choice among the candidates for the full position—Truck was really Coach Washburn's only hope—and there's not one chance in a million of finding another fullback at this late date."

"How about using halfbacks?" said Gerry. Then in reply to Tom's puzzled frown, he explained, "One halfback plus one halfback equals one fullback. Simple problem in mathematics."

"Somebody choke him," Tom suggested. "No, but seriously, can't something be done to make Truck come alive and get interested in football? Man, if that fellow would get really mad just once, there'd be fireworks and to spare. But you couldn't get a rise out of him with an elevator. He just gives you a sweet smile and plods on peacefully."

"With Guinevere," said Jimmy Carlton, joining the discussion.

"Oh, yes, Guinevere," said Hugh, even more gloomily than before. "I'd forgotten Guinevere."

Gerry roused himself from a lethargy. "That's the famous white mouse, isn't it?" he asked. "Do you know I've never seen the animal?"

"Never seen Guinevere?" Jimmy stared at his teammate in incredulous surprise. "Never seen that superb, divine, and altogether marvelous representative of the genus mouse?" Gerry shook his head. "Such things must not be," said Jimmy and dashed wildly to the other end of the long locker room, returning a moment later with Truck Baker in tow.

The fullback thoroughly deserved his sobriquet of Truck, solid and square as he was, weighing close to a hundred and ninety-five and standing a little over five feet ten. He was a placid, blond giant who rarely spoke and then only after serious thought and contemplation. Now he stood and regarded Gerry with solemn intensity and interest.

"Gerry," said Jimmy by way of explanation, "has never seen Guinevere."

Truck's face suddenly lighted in happy anticipation. He shot a huge paw out and gripped Gerry by the elbow, dragging him toward the door with no verbal comment. Gerry, wholly unable to cope with an irresistible force, meekly allowed himself to be propelled through the door, across the field and up the steps of Blaisdell Hall before he ventured a remark.

"Where *are* we going?" he asked.

Truck did not waste words but pushed Gerry through a dark corridor, into a room and onto a chair where he suddenly and inexplicably deserted him. Gerry gazed about in bewilderment and was relieved when his host reappeared, carrying a small box. This he presented to Gerry with the air of quiet pride habitually worn by magicians who produce rabbits from silk hats.

Gerry accepted the box silently and peered within. A small white mouse reposed peacefully on a cottonwool bed and regarded him with beady eyes. "And this," said Gerry, "is Guinevere?"

"That's Guinevere," said Truck, as one might say, "That's the Parthenon."

Gerry gazed at the white mouse reverently; the white mouse gazed back at him more or less irreverently. "Why Guinevere?" said Gerry.

"Because that's her name," Truck explained.

"I see. The mouse is named Guinevere because Guinevere is the name of the mouse."

"Yes," said Truck.

Gerry glanced at him quickly, then back at Guinevere. "It's very beautiful," he said in a curiously choked voice, handing the box back to its owner. "Very, very beautiful. Thank you for letting me see it. I shall—" he paused and coughed—"always remember this moment."

"You're quite welcome," Truck said in all seriousness. "Sorry you have to go. See you tomorrow."

Gerry let himself out the front door quietly, then collapsed gurgling on the steps. Hugh detached himself from a tree and crossed the street to Gerry's side, laying a soothing hand on his friend's shoulder.

"There, there," said Hugh. "I know how it is. I felt that way, too, the first time, but I got over it."

Gerry straightened up and wiped his eyes. "G-G-Guinevere," he sputtered, and dissolved again into fresh spasms of mirth.

"Guinevere," said Hugh sadly. "Our big bad fullback's one interest in life, his one enthusiasm—a white mouse. For the love of Mike—" he exploded suddenly in righteous indignation—"I could bear a dog or something, but a white mouse—"

"A dog might be worse," Gerry pointed out, "following him around and everything."

"Yes, but a dog's a dog and—"

"Well, a mouse is a mouse," said Gerry reasonably. "And, after all, few white mouses—mice, I mean—are named Guinevere. That, you'll admit, is a distinction."

"Distinction, nuts," Hugh growled. "If Truck would show one-tenth the interest in the team that he does in his darned old Guinevere, we might win a game this season. For the love of lemons, Gerry, can't anything be done to make that guy wake up and do something?"

Gerry shook his head sadly. "Honest to Pete, I don't see a ray of hope. Coach is sick about it and I don't blame him. It wouldn't be so maddening if Truck wasn't such marvelous material—he's sort of a composite portrait of everything a fullback should be—only he just sits there and acts pleasant. Heck, in the Bayliss game he practically apologized to the runner every time he made a tackle."

"Well, do something about it," said Hugh impatiently. "You're always such an old fixit, here's your chance. Make Truck come to and play football what is football, and you can have half my kingdom and both my neckties."

"I'll make a mental note of the matter," Gerry promised, walking off in the direction of his rooms.

"That's the trouble with you," Hugh shouted after him scathingly. "You write things down in your mind, and then you lose your head."

A discouraged-looking eleven trailed slowly off the field at the end of the Parker-Fayfield game and straggled listlessly into the Parker quarters. Jimmy Carlton sank on a bench with a mournful grunt and tossed his helmet to the floor. "Thirteen to nothing," he said to no one in particular.

"Thirteen to nothing," Gerry agreed, staring vacantly into space and wrestling absently with a shoelace. "And it might as easily have been thirty to nothing, for all the competition we gave 'em. The line was as limp as a dishrag. And I'm not saying that just because I'm in the backfield either," he added hastily.

"No?" said Jimmy, temporarily indignant but too tired to carry the fight into enemy territory. "Oh, well, I'll have to admit that the line was a bit sloppy." He lowered his voice cautiously. "But I won't admit that the backfield covered itself with glory because, old trout, it most certainly didn't. What, for instance, about our playful little fullback and his great big boner in the fourth quarter?"

"His fumble, you mean?" said Gerry.

"What do you think he means?" Hugh chimed in irritably. "His fumble and a few other little trifles, such as not knowing what down it was. Truck trotted around all through the game, just as gentle and sweet and happy as a lamb prancing in the buttercups. Just out for the fresh air, Truck was, that's all. Football? Pooh-pooh and tush-tush. A great big rough game like that, when the birdies are singing and the white mice are scampering and—"

"Control yourself," said Gerry firmly, effectively spiking his friend's tirade with one elbow in his ribs. "It gets you nowhere—as I dashed well know by experience—and anyhow, for once Truck is not so well pleased with his own performance. Take a look." He jerked a thumb toward the rear of the room where the fullback sat, wrapped in gloom and a blue blanket.

"Does look a bit miffed," said Jimmy thoughtfully.

"He ought to," Hugh maintained.

"Is it possible," said Gerry, "that Truck is actually feeling twinges of repentance for a misspent life? Is he, in fact, sorry that we lost a game? Does he—can he—be thinking that he's more or less to blame?"

"But is he to blame?" Jimmy protested.

"Ye-es, I think so. He was definitely the weak spot, and Fayfield knew it. He just hasn't got any fight, and you can't get around it, Jimmy. Hugh's right, much as I hate to admit it. Don't tell him I said so," he added hastily. "He's quite vain enough as it is."

Hugh acknowledged his insult with a dirty look and relapsed into a gloomy silence again. Gerry went on blissfully. "Truck shouldn't take it too hard, though," he pointed out. "A little worry won't hurt him, but we don't want him thinking he's no good at all. He might leave the team and then we'd be in a sweet pickle."

"I don't like sweet pickles," said Jimmy.

"Neither do I," Gerry agreed amiably, "and therefore I'm going over and cheer Truckykins up. I shall scatter sweetness and light and—"

"I don't care what you scatter," said Hugh coldly. "Just scatter, and I'll be satisfied."

Gerry obediently scattered and crossed to Truck, greeting him with a hearty slap on the shoulder. "Cheer up, old scout," he said brightly. "It's not that bad."

Truck heaved a sigh that came from the cellar. "It's worse," he said.

Gerry sat down. "It's not altogether your fault," he pointed out. "I suppose in a way you did your best."

"It *is* my fault," said Truck. "Entirely mine. You're right, though. I *did* do my best. I couldn't help—"

Gerry thought of the fumble. "No, I suppose not. I wasn't thinking of that, really. I was thinking more of your not knowing about the down—or forgetting—or whatever it was you did."

Truck looked up from a preoccupied study of his knuckles. "Not down," he said. "Fur."

Gerry looked at him curiously. "What do you mean—*fur?*" he inquired.

"It's called fur, not down. Down is what birds have. Mice have *fur.*" Truck was very patient in his explanation.

Gerry swallowed hard and fixed Truck with a glittering eye. It was a few moments before he could trust himself to speak. When he did, his words were very measured and slow. "May one be permitted to ask what in the name of pink turtles you're talking about?"

Truck looked at him innocently and with the utmost candor. "Guinevere," he said simply. "I thought you knew—she's molting."

* * * * *

There was nothing in the prospects of the Richmond game to excite much enthusiasm or hope on the part of the Parker student body, comparative scores and records giving Richmond a sizable advantage, but the entire school nevertheless turned out loyally for one of the most famous traditional battles in the league. Granted that Parker stood small chance of even a tie, the two teams always put up a good scrap and you never could tell what might happen. Anyhow, the cheering would be good and the weather was nice. So ran the thoughts of the Parker rooters, and by game time the stands were a solid mass of gay colors, with Parker blue and Richmond green predominating.

In the Parker locker room, however, there was no such cheerfulness or festivity. The gloom, as Coach Washburn pointed out, could be cut with a knife, and not a particularly sharp knife at that; and what little team spirit had up to now existed was quietly ebbing away. The only happy and contented figures in the whole scene of woe were those of Truck and Guinevere, his pet having been unofficially introduced as team mascot. Guinevere watched proceedings from a cage on top of a locker, and Truck watched Guinevere. Coach Washburn for the two-hundredth time that afternoon looked at the wide shoulders and muscular, thick-set frame of his fullback, looked at the tiny restless mouse, and sighed deeply.

"All right, gang," he barked, simulating a false enthusiasm and cheer. "Get in there and fight. Remember—no game's lost until the last gun. Now get going, fellows, and show me what you can do."

The team nodded dutifully if incredulously and trotted through the open door, helmets swinging, to be greeted by wave upon wave of frantic cheering from the Parker stands. Somewhat heartened, Hugh glanced at Gerry. "You know we might win at that, if a bomb exploded under Truck."

"I'm not an army," said Gerry. "I have no bombs."

Both teams warmed up for a few minutes, and Gerry hastily appraised their opponents. His heart sank into his kangaroo leather shoes as he contemplated Richmond's fullback, Pudge Lorrimer. "Big as Truck—faster, probably—handles himself like a blooming piledriver—fighting face—ugh," the captain summed him up mentally and longed for Hugh's bomb. The referee's whistle interrupted his fruitless yearnings.

Within five minutes, it was perfectly apparent to the supporters of the blue that they had little, if anything, to cheer about. Pudge Lorrimer with monotonous regularity broke great holes in the Parker line, through which slipped Richmond backs to click off smooth five- and ten-yard gains. Heroic tackling in the secondary defense prevented any of these gains from material-izing into touchdown runs, but the deadly precision of consecutive downs forced Parker into the shadow of their own goal posts early in the first quar-ter. There the Richmond quarterback with cool judgment ordered Pudge into opposing full, and in two bone-crushing plunges, Pudge made the necessary yardage by the simple method of bowling Truck out of the way and replacing him with the ball. Truck apparently did not resent this summary treatment, but the rest of the team did, and loud mutters of unrest rose in increasing volume throughout the rest of the period.

Pudge missed the extra point, and, when the whistle ended the first quar-ter, the ball was already on Parker's thirty in Richmond's possession. Rich-mond scored once more before the end of the half, and Teddy Page, Parker quarterback, finally realizing the futility of giving Truck the ball, satisfied himself with end runs, off-tackle slants, and much vigorous kicking. His re-ward for this caution was an unchanged score of 12 to 0 when the gun ended the half, and the teams left the field.

In the locker room, Coach Washburn for the first time in his career blew sky-high, concentrating his attack on Truck, who regarded him with patient bewilderment. After five solid minutes of expressing himself, the coach saw that he was getting nowhere bucking against a brick wall, and finally gave up for lack of breath. Gerry, who had been trying for some time to stem the tor-rent, burst out with a wild yell.

"It's gone!" said Gerry. "It's gone!"

Everyone swung in his direction to find him pointing frenziedly to the top of a locker, on which reposed an empty cage.

"Guinevere!" yelled Truck and took two benches in his stride to reach the cage. "She's gone!"

"Really?" said Jimmy. "That's bad."

Teddy looked thoroughly bewildered. "But Gerry opened the door himself—" he began, when an accurately thrown shoe struck his shoulder and silenced him.

"Gerry what?" said Truck, swinging about and regarding his teammates truculently.

"You silly fool," Gerry hissed into Teddy's ear, "why can't you keep your mouth shut?" He turned to Truck nervously. "Teddy means I opened the outside door—left it open, I mean—when I came in. I was the last one in, you know, and I left it open. He means that Guinevere may have gotten outside. Don't you, Teddy?" He regarded Teddy with a sweet smile and kicked him forcefully on the shin. Teddy said Yes, that was what he had meant.

"Help me find her," said Truck desperately, getting down on his knees and crawling under a bench in anxious search. "She may still be here. I can't see—" he wailed. "I can't see how the cage door got open!"

"By cracky!"

"By my sainted aunt!"

Hugh and Gerry appeared to have been struck by the same thought. Hugh spoke first. "I *thought* I saw someone slip out the side door. It's just dawned on me." He turned to Gerry. "Didn't you?" Gerry nodded grimly. "That's it, I'll bet a cookie," Hugh pursued this theme excitedly. "Don't you remember last year when we got the Richmond mascot just before the big game—that rooster, you know. Well, they're paying us back, that's what. They've kidnapped Guinevere."

"Kidnapped Guinevere!" Truck howled. "Kidnapped Guinevere? You mean they've taken her—the Richmond fellows?"

"That's it," said Gerry solemnly. "That's it, all right. Pretty slick, eh? Well, it's tough, but I guess turnabout's fair play. We took their rooster—they take our mouse."

"But," Truck expostulated wildly, "their rooster was only a rooster, but our mouse was—Guinevere." He cast another wild glance around the room and looked under a helmet.

Gerry took his arm gently. "No use looking here. They won't have let Guinevere out," he said. "They'll have taken it—her—with them. She's probably in their locker room now."

"I'll raid it," Truck threatened. "I'll tear it apart! I'll show them they can't kidnap Guinevere. Why, she's delicate and she has to be fed regularly. She—she—" He lapsed into incoherent sputters.

"It's tough, old man," said Gerry. "We'll get her back all right, but just now we've got to get onto the field." He turned to Hugh. "Who was it you thought you saw outside the building?"

"Well—" Hugh paused for dramatic effect— "I'd hate to accuse anybody, but it certainly looked like Pudge Lorrimer."

"He'd have had to travel pretty darn fast to get here before we did," objected Teddy, apparently bent on being difficult and getting his shin kicked again for his pains.

Truck ignored him. "Pudge Lorrimer, huh?" he panted. "Just you wait till I lay my hands on that guy. I'll tear him to pieces. I'll wrap him around the goal posts. I'll—"

"Come on," said Hugh soothingly, dragging the fullback away. "I quite agree with you." He shoved him through the door and the rest of the team followed.

Gerry paused for a moment and thrust something into the coach's hands. "For the love of lemons," he muttered frantically, "take this darned animal and keep it. Easy now." Coach Washburn accepted Guinevere in a dazed silence and stowed her away in a capacious pocket. As Gerry went out, a slow, wide smile dawned on the coach's face.

* * * * *

"Atta boy, Truck! Eat 'em up!" The Parker stands rose to their feet as one man, as the revived blue team swept up the field. Truck hugging the ball and bowling aside would-be interference.

"He's gone mad," said a reporter in the quiet, plaintive way reporters have, and made a note to that effect on the paper before him. There was certainly no other explanation of Truck's merciless attack, of the incredible slashing touchdown march which had made the score 12 to 7, of what was being done to Pudge Lorrimer, who was showing distinct signs of wear.

"Great mackerel," said Hugh aside to Gerry, "it's sure working."

"Praises be, he's sticking to football for revenge and didn't start a prize-fight," said Gerry thankfully. "I've been sitting on the edge of a volcano."

"You're still there," said Hugh.

The whistle shrilled, the teams lined up. Teddy barked out signals, and Truck hit the line with a resounding smack for three yards. When the referee untangled the pileup, Tom Martin stayed stretched out on the ground. An official bent over him anxiously.

"He's all right," said Tom weakly. "Wind knocked out."

Coach Washburn came out quickly from the sidelines and crossed to the stricken tackle. Tom repeated his assertion and struggled to a sitting position. The coach bent over him. . . .

A waving whisker poked cautiously out of the coach's pocket, followed by a sleek white head. There was a convulsive wiggle, and a second later Guinevere popped out of her prison and started hastily across the field. Truck permitted one wild whoop to escape him before he dashed in reckless pursuit with half the team after him. Guinevere was captured on the ten-yard line and brought back, panting and subdued in her master's hands. In speechless indignation and fury, Truck regarded Hugh and Gerry.

"I—" Gerry began.

"He—" Hugh began.

Truck silenced them with a magnificent gesture. "You—peanuts," he said superbly and started off the field. Coach Washburn grabbed him by his wrist and hauled him back.

"You can't leave like that," said the coach reasonably.

"I am leaving," said Truck with cold dignity.

"You can't," said the coach helplessly.

"Let's get on with the game," said Pudge Lorrimer.

Truck saw him for the first time as an individual and not as something to be knocked over. "I owe you an apology," he said. "They—" he pointed at Hugh and Gerry—"they told me you kidnaped Guinevere. I'm sorry I believed them."

"Guinevere?" said Pudge. "Oh, you mean your mouse. Great guns, no, I wouldn't take your mouse. I like them—have two of my own, in fact. Cute little beggars—about *so* big." He measured their size between thumb and forefinger.

"You have two white mice?" said Truck happily. "Tell me something, old man. Do they molt?"

"Shed fur?" said Pudge. "Sure they do. What you want to give them then is—"

At this point the referee took matters into his own hands. "What about the game?" he said.

Reluctantly, Pudge dropped the matter of white mice and strolled into position. Truck, still seething with wrath against his teammates and full of affection for a fellow mouse-lover, relinquished Guinevere reluctantly to a cheerleader's tender mercies and got into the lineup. The interrupted game continued.

Truck, no longer on speaking terms with anyone in the backfield and few people in the line, and having no grudge whatever against his adversaries, returned to his usual football style. Pudge, untrammeled by sentiment and keeping his mice apart from his football, also played his usual game. The result was an unchanged score in the fourth quarter, thanks only to desperate stonewall defenses on Parker's part, but Richmond once more held the ball on Parker's ten and the line was crumbling under the severe treatment being doled out to it. Truck was frankly no longer interested. He carried the ball when it was given to him, but that was all.

Parker got to its first break of the day when the Richmond center fumbled on the eight-yard line, giving the ball to the blue. Teddy called for a kick and prayed that Gerry would get it off.

Signals were given, the ball was snapped back, the green line swarmed in to block the kick. Gerry hadn't a chance as the line broke. Without stopping to think, he whirled and thrust the pigskin into Truck's unwilling hands. Truck backed away from the attackers, instinctively dodged a green-jerseyed guard—

And there Guinevere took matters into her own paws. She had escaped from the cheerleader some minutes before, but that person had thought it wise not to mention the matter. Consequently, just as Gerry thrust the ball upon Truck, Guinevere attained the Parker twenty-yard line. A friendly animal, she advanced upon the host, unaware that cleated shoes and weighty linesmen were apt to be damaging to the most ferocious of white mice.

When Truck saw her, she was on the fifteen, mincing lightheartedly along and pausing only to sniff delicately at bits of clover. Truck let out the howl which was becoming a slogan with him and bounded forward. "Look out!" he shouted. "You'll be stepped on!" Like a madman he raced to the rescue of his precious pet. Guinevere backed off hastily, unaccustomed as she was to being addressed in this manner. The Richmond defense swung in pursuit of Truck, Truck pounded after Guinevere, Guinevere frankly turned tail and ran for her life.

"Epic," was one reporter's adjective; "colossal and unbelievable," another's. Still a third said simply, "The greatest run I have ever seen." Richmond players were entirely ignored or pushed heartily in the face by the now thoroughly maniacal Truck in his headlong dash for Guinevere and, incidentally, the goal posts, though they occupied no place in his thoughts. Gerry, knocked down en route and used as a doormat by practically the whole Richmond team, sat up dizzily and prayed that Truck would hang on to the ball.

Truck did. As he crossed the goal line, two yards ahead of the nearest Richmond pursuer, the Parker stands went crazy mad; the referee's hands shot up over his head; the band burst into "Three Cheers for Parker," and Coach Washburn staggered back to the bench and sat on the superintendent's hat. Truck, totally unaware of these proceedings, rushed on, nor did he achieve his aim until some thirty yards beyond the goal posts, where Guinevere gave up and sat down on the grass.

Truck scooped her up and walked back toward the field, the ball still under his arm. Jimmy Carlton met him, relieved him of its weight and gently touched it down behind the white stripes of the enemy goal. The scoreboard read Parker 13, Richmond 12.

The referee mopped his brow. "The longest run I've ever witnessed," he said weakly.

Hugh and Gerry rushed forward and seized upon Truck with enthusiasm. "Great stuff, old man," said Gerry. "That's the most corking run I've ever seen!"

"Oh, that's nothing," said Truck, beaming modestly. "You should see her sometimes in the hallway."

* * * * *

"Guinevere, the Mouse," by B. J. Chute. Published in St. Nicholas, *November 1934. Original text owned by Joe Wheeler. B. J. Chute of Minneapolis was a prolific author of books and short stories during much of the twentieth century. Some of her books include* Greenwillow, The Blue Cup and Other Stories, *and* Blocking Back.

The Smart Little "Wassup"

Percy S. Wheaton

All animals—large and small—in the wild find it difficult to survive. Always there is danger at every turn.
Even for the tiny wasp.

* * * * *

Old Major, the horse, had gone to sleep, and I was about to arouse him, when, *Bing!* A digger wasp flew past my ear so close and so fast that I was afraid I had disturbed her preserve.

However, knowing something of her habits, I sat perfectly still, believing that even if I had offended her, she wouldn't attempt to avenge herself unless I started the fight. She circled around three or four times and finally alighted by a little stone, almost within arm's reach, and deposited a paralyzed spider beside it.

She flicked her wings and preened herself. She examined the little stone and appeared excited over something. She walked in ever-widening circles around the stone and, finally, taking wing, extended the limits of her investigation. Having satisfied herself that her fears had been groundless, she flew back and settled once more beside the little stone. She seized it in her jaws and, assisting with one forefoot, lifted it bodily to one side (the stone must have been far heavier than the wasp herself), and displayed to my astonished gaze a hole in the hard earth, cleanly cut and about the size of a small slate pencil.

She peeked into the hole, evidently still suspicious. She stuck her head in the hole and withdrew it. Then she felt all around the edges of the hole and rubbed the rough spots. Being satisfied that all was right, she began again to preen herself. This being done, she backed up to the hole, smoothed her wings flat, and backed down into the ground completely out of sight. A minute later she reappeared, picked up the paralyzed spider, and, again, smoothing her wings, once more backed into the hole carrying the spider with her.

This time she was gone much longer. When she reappeared, she repeated the circling performance, even giving a threatening buzz at my hat to make sure I was either dead or harmless. She realighted by the hole, lifted the stone and covered it, and then, standing upon the stone, scratched, cat fashion, in all directions, finishing the job by blowing the dust to every point of the compass with short blasts from her wings. Again she circled and investigated, and, finally, satisfied that her strategy had been infallible, flew away.

All the while I had been watching her, I had been thinking. I remembered the little partridges I had surprised in an open place. Experience had taught me to watch one chicken and not the flock; but even then, when a baby partridge had grasped an oak leaf—and that oak leaf not more than six feet from me—and had turned on his back dragging the leaf over him, I never was able to find him under that leaf. Only once did I have anything like success, and that success was attained by long, patient, silent, waiting.

So, as I sat watching this wasp, I wondered if she could so disguise the stone that covered the hole that I could not find it. Not that I contemplated any injury to her or hers, but rather that I wished to prove the quality of her work. Therefore, I sat with my gaze glued upon that stone, and, after she had

flown away, I dropped forward on my hands and knees—mind you, never looking anywhere else but at that stone—and picked it up, expecting to see the little hole under it. *And it was the wrong stone.*

Carefully replacing it, I as carefully lifted every other stone within a foot radius. Still no hole. I lifted these stones by gripping the edges with my nails, lifting them only far enough to peek under them. I examined the adjacent ground for signs. It was all uniformly hard and bare. I never showed anyone that wasp's hole-in-the-ground, because, though I knew where it was, I couldn't find it.

Here was the thing about it all that struck me most forcibly. There I sat within five or six feet of the base of operations, and still, by making use of all my powers, was unable to locate the exact spot. There I was, supposed to be one of the lords of creation, capable of reasoning and deduction; and still had been completely fooled by a mere wasp.

She had first prepared the hole and cover, selecting a place where there were a vast number of similar stones to confuse all her enemies. Then she had flown away to a distance which, if we compare her weight to ours, would have amounted to several thousand miles, to search for her legitimate prey. Having secured it, she returned unerringly and alighted on the *right side* of the right stone.

* * * * *

At the time of the next incident related here, I was working near a veranda step having at least five stairs. Both the veranda and the steps were equipped with a high, solid rail, which arrangement left a high and deep corner for shrubbery. For some reason the one corner was partly bare, and a huge spider had selected this place as a proper spot to lay a snare for the unwary.

He was a fat old devil, cocksure and domineering, and had the habit of dashing across the web, lifting his prey bodily, and carrying it to his corner nest for leisurely disposal. He was so big that he had forgotten what caution or fear meant. He could easily have carried a lightning bug or a snapping beetle, and I wouldn't have been surprised to have seen him pick up a June bug and walk off with it. He was a bloody old ogreish butcher, if there ever was one; but I didn't interfere with his occupation, partly because he was interesting, partly because he destroyed flies and mosquitoes, and partly because I believe it unwise to interfere with nature's balances unless necessity compels it.

So, on this day being near his den, I was more or less keeping an eye on him, when a wasp suddenly came and alighted in the middle of the web. Instantly, Mr. Spider rushed and struck. There was a flash of brownish-gray spider and a plaintively buzzing and much-entangled wasp one instant, and in the next began a battle royal such as I never expect to see again.

The spider must have outweighed the wasp six to one; and yet that wasp jumped eagerly and confidently into the conflict. But the battle was too unequal. The tremendous bulk of the spider required more venom to paralyze it than the wasp was able to inject. In spite of the spider's best efforts to tear himself loose, the wasp clinched and struck again and again. Six times I counted, she drove her poisoned lance into the abdomen and thorax of the huge spider, meanwhile fighting him tooth and toe nail to keep his killing jaws away from her throat; for this fight was face to face and the wasp had no opportunity to place her stab, as she usually did, somewhere in what serves the spider for a spinal system.

In the meantime, the spider had not been idle. His instinct to enshroud his prey showed itself even in the heat of battle, for, as he took the vicious stabs, each one of which convulsed him, he was busy winding leg and wing of the wasp, and tying the loose ends fast to the web. Finally, convinced of the futility of further battle, the spider made one supreme convulsive effort and tore himself loose from the grasp of that living death. Retiring to the edge of his den, he began to bite himself, first in one leg joint and then in another, until he had bitten every joint that he could reach.

The wasp was thoroughly enmeshed. Her day was done and she knew it. She made neither struggle nor protest when the spider again approached her. Stepping warily, with one eye apparently cocked for trouble, he circled the wasp several times, laying a path of new threads as a sort of sidewalk from which he could work to better advantage. Then, reaching as far as he could, he began to fasten web all over the most extended portions of the wasp with quick spatting blows. His caution was almost comical. He would prepare a strand of web, then jump, spat, and jump back. He reminded me of a cat I once saw testing the deadness of a water moccasin.

Next, the spider floated strands of web across the wasp and made a detour to fasten them. It must have taken him nearly fifteen minutes to make sure of his work. He even swathed the wasp's abdomen and guyed the stinger end and upper thorax so tightly that the wasp could not have curled up to sting under any circumstances.

But the spider by no means got off scot-free. Contrary to his usual procedure, he made no attempt to eat his catch. Instead, he crawled to the edge of his nest and again proceeded to bite his joints. He reminded me of Giant Despair, and Giant Despair he was; for, when I returned that evening, the spider lay curled in his last long sleep, that living death to which the virus of the wasp condemns all spiders.

* * * * *

The scene now shifts and the time is the present year. I had just stepped out of the house and stood pondering whether I would take my daily walk up or down the street, when the hum of a wasp attracted me.

She dodged hither and yon, circled my head twice, and finally settled in the center of a spider's web. She buzzed like an airplane, and I was on the point of helping her out, when the spider made a valiant rush to secure, if possible, this huge prey before it had opportunity to escape. The thing was too easy, but not according to the spider's calculations. The wasp maintained her frightened buzzing until the spider was in easy reach. Then, suddenly seizing him, she first bit and then stung him, and then, spreading her wings, easily broke the strand or two that held her and flew away with her prize.

And so a thought comes to me. *Could the wasp that flew into the web in the corner of the porch have been playing the same kind of a game?* I remember now, there was a little spider that built his nest in the corner above the other—a little web and built in such a shape it did not interfere with the big spider. I remember wondering at the time why the big spider didn't chase him out; for I have even seen him get small insects out of the big spider's web. Could that wasp have had her eye on that little spider and intended to pick him for her victim? Did she drop down there expecting to catch a cat and find a tiger instead? At least the wasp fought a willing and valiant battle against tremendous odds, and lost—and won.

* * * * *

"The Smart Little 'Wassup,' " by Percy S. Wheaton. Published in St. Nicholas, *September 1934. Original text owned by Joe Wheeler. Percy S. Wheaton wrote for popular magazines during the first half of the twentieth century.*

AMELIA, THE FLYING SQUIRREL

Alexander Sprunt Jr.

For the animals that lived there in the cypress swamps, death lurked in trees, in shrubs, in inky pools—but their greatest fear was reserved for fire!

* * * * *

It was dark; a pitchy, impenetrable blackness lay over the low-country woods like an almost palpable blanket. It was quiet too; a stillness so profound that it vied with the darkness in intensity, for there was no wind. Suddenly, amid the all-enveloping gloom, appeared two points of palely glowing light. They came from nowhere, seemingly; one moment they had not been there, the next, they were flaring greenly, steadily fixed, with a strange, unwavering intensity in their depths.

Then a sound broke the stillness; only a little one, a tiny scratching, as of infinitesimal claws on bark. The green points seemed to flicker, only to blaze out again in a renewed brilliance. As the sound continued, a pale, silvery glow grew over the forest. The moon had come, and coincident with its advent those sinister balls of flame crept forward, then shot through space with incredible swiftness. A pounce and a growl followed; a big, dark shape bunched upon a high limb, as from under it leaped a tiny object silhouetted against the moon's gleam; a fleeting shadow that was instantly lost in the deep gloom beneath the trees.

Behind it, on the limb, the wildcat vented its disappointed rage in a high-pitched, piercing scream that ran eerily over the silent forest and sleeping swamp, to sink in far-reaching echoes across the tidal river.

* * * * *

The low-country day was drawing to a close. The glow in the western sky faded slowly, while the stars grew brighter amid the evening stillness; the old pine towered blackly against the steely heavens, huge and gaunt, a monumental silhouette. Dead it was; a stark and bleached remnant of a pineland monarch, but that it still harbored life within its scarred and furrowed trunk was beyond all doubting.

Just before darkness fell, a tiny head appeared in a crevice far up on that lofty shaft. A pair of sparkling eyes gazed out over the somber cypress swamp; eyes that held in their liquid depths an eager, inquisitive scrutiny of the quiet scene below. Down there the activities of the furred and feathered folk were lessening; the time of rest had come for many—but not for all. For others, the time of rest had passed, and their day was only starting.

Behind the eager eyes, large ears twitched quickly as a sound floated upward to the little watcher; a chuck-will's-widow in a live oak began its evening chant in clear-cut, clacking notes. Amelia listened to the bird for a moment, then emerged from her hollow and squatted on a short, knotted limb that protruded from the trunk immediately below the crevice. Seen from below, she would have seemed but another knot upon the branch, for she was very small. Like many things, however, Amelia would not have suffered from close inspection. She was of an exquisite delicacy in appearance: her body clothed in soft, silky fur of a slate color; the sides of head and neck were cream, while beneath she was snowy white.

In one particular characteristic, Amelia was unique among the wild kindred of the low country. It was no so much her daintiness of form, striking as that was, nor was it her abnormally large and intelligent eyes. It was the presence of a thin, flexible membrane covered with the finest fur, similar in color to her body, that extended from her forelegs to the hind, on each flank. This membrane was edged with cream and clung closely to her sides in a beautiful scalloped border. Her tail was nearly as long as her body and arched gracefully over her back as she sat quietly on the limb, gazing into the rapidly gathering gloom. Amelia was a flying squirrel.

It was May in the low country and the sunset, dying behind the cypress swamp, was a lovely benediction to the day. A faint odor floated upward to the squirrel's perch, a combination of sweet myrtle, wood violets, and aromatic pine needles. Amelia sniffed the wandering air currents as the light breeze sighed about the pine, and as she did so, a tiny squeak sounded from the dark hollow behind her. Instantly she whirled and darted inward, to fondle two little balls of fur upon the chips that lined the bottom of the cavity; then she emerged once more, alert and active.

A passing nighthawk twanged by the pine, and Amelia left the limb in a long drop, her membrane spread like a miniature parachute, and in a graceful, noiseless swoop, she glided toward the invisible ground. Shooting swiftly along, she neared a stump about a yard in height, straightened out her course, and with a slight upward impetus, came to rest upon it. Standing erect, she glanced sharply about her and ran nimbly to the ground to forage busily in the grasses.

As she worked she kept constant vigil; her vision, wonderfully acute in the gloom, pierced the leafy coverts on all sides as she captured insect larvae, picked up seeds, and cracked an occasional nut. She was perfectly able to take care of herself without such intense care, but she wanted no such narrow escape as had been hers the night before, when the wildcat had attempted to leap upon her in the oak. She had won free, but only by a hair, for the cat's claws had all but pinned her to the bark. Too much depended on her for any chance-taking; the little bundles of fur back in the old pine were yet blind and helpless; she must hunt and eat, but she must need to be very careful.

Her vigilance, keen as it was, did not save her and her little ones that night, however. It was something else, a thing as unlooked for and quick as the murderous attack upon herself. Four eyes had watched Amelia when she sailed up to the stump and ran down it into the grasses; eyes that had in them a greedy light of anticipation and expectancy. They followed her as she neared a clump of broom grass near the woods' edge; then one pair of eyes wavered from her and turned themselves upon the other watcher.

Amelia saw the danger too late to do anything to ward it off; it was the all but inaudible whisper of a shaken grass stem that caused her to whirl about and see the slim weasel almost upon her. She could not jump, and so she flattened herself instinctively. It was the only thing to do. The brown marauder had overestimated his distance slightly and landed squarely atop the crouching Amelia, covering her with his body. Then, before he could whirl about and gain a hold, a kind of flicker appeared behind; what seemed to be a slender rod emerged from the broom-grass clump like a flash of darting light, barely touched the weasel's side, and was instantly withdrawn.

The effect on the animal was electric. A sharp squeal split the stillness, and the furry body fell sideways. Amelia, relieved of its weight, acted on the moment. A supple spring shot her away from the squirming shape of her attacker, and in another bound she reached the stump. Flashing over it, she darted through the grasses, scurried like a streak across the open, and ascended the old pine like a fleeting shadow. Behind her, the weasel stretched out at full length, gave a jerky kick or two, and sank into a limp heap. Quiet reigned for several moments; then from the grass clump came a long, sinuous, gliding shape that circled about the still form, the slender forked tongue flicking from its triangular head. High up in the old pine, meanwhile, Amelia fed her hungry youngsters, snuggled them up to her, and settled down in restful contentment as the moon came up over the cypress swamp.

When the little ones were sound asleep, Amelia crept silently to the entrance and took up her position again upon the stub just below it. The moon made a glory of the woods as she sat there; the blackly soaring columns of the tree trunks were etched in statuesque massiveness against a delicate tracery of light and shadow; the swaying banners of moss caught the pale sheen in shifting, ghostly shimmerings, and the glint of the water in the nearby lagoon was as bright and metallic as hammered silver. The little watcher on the stub, however, was looking for other things than the fantastic play of the shadows beneath her. Work was over for a time, and it was the hour of play; she wanted company—and it was not long in coming.

From another trunk not far away, a tiny shape swooped downward on a long slant, disappeared, and reappeared against the black and silver background, to alight, fifty yards distant, upon a stump and jerk upright in alert reconnaissance of its surroundings. Another swooped from a second tree, then two from a third, while the first darted over the grass, climbed upward, and sailed again. More came until there were a dozen, and their aerial swoops became weaving threads from tree to tree. Amelia was in the midst of the happy band, glorying in the swift drop, the long sail, and the little upward zoom at the ground to a resting place. It was as though a company of woods' sprites were holding festival beneath the silent play of the moonbeams, and the tiny revelers were as quiet in their fun as the moon-bathed night itself.

Up, down, up again, and down once more they went, never resting, until a sudden shadow fell upon the grasses by the rim of the clearing. Wide wings, soundless as a falling leaf, winnowed over the playground; two yellow eyes glared from a tufted head; two armored feet shot outward from a fluffy, feathered body, as a great horned owl burst in upon the aerial party. There was a frantic scrambling; a shooting of tiny shapes hither and thither, a muffled squeak, and the silent marauder passed on, leaving behind an empty clearing. High up in the old pine Amelia gazed philosophically into the shades whence the owl had disappeared, then turned inward. For that night the play was over.

It was a memorable day for Amelia when her youngsters, with much scrambling and falling backward, finally gained the entrance to their home and emerged to squat upon the stub. With eyes bulging in amazed wonder, they stared down from their lofty station over a scene that the sinking sun painted with a hazy sheen of gold. It was still, and the leaves stirred but slightly in the soft breeze, a gentle breath that was as soothing as the play of changing color in the sky. The little animated smudges of fur clung tightly to the weathered wood, guarded by the proud mother in adoring solicitude as she watched the varied emotions come and go in their large, dark eyes.

The evening star blazed brilliantly in the background of illimitable space above, and seemed to draw their gaze like a magnet. While shifting interested glances downward to the gathering shadows under the pine, their eyes turned always back to that silently glittering point of light. The tiny membranes, still unable to support them, lay folded closely along their sides, rimming each one with a delicate, creamy-bordered shawl, and bringing out the exquisite shade of the silky fur above and below in contrasting tones of gray and white. For perhaps a quarter of an hour, they remained in wondering scrutiny, their heads twisting about, and an occasional creeping movement changing their hold upon the stub. Then Amelia, with gentle squeaks of command, ushered them back into the black hollow, and scrambling safely inward, they snuggled to her in little wriggling movements of satisfaction, somewhat awed by the vastness of the world without, and experiencing a sense of restful contentment in the narrow confines of their snug, dark home.

They grew steadily, thriving upon abundant food, and the daily excursions to the perch outside became a regular part of their routine. One of the youngsters, more precocious than the other, would make his way outward considerably before sunset, while Amelia was yet asleep.

For a day or so this program was pursued tranquilly enough. Then, one afternoon, Amelia was awakened by a sharp and appealing little cry. Instantly alert, she jerked upward and saw but one of her progeny beside her. In a flash she leaped for the entrance, to behold the venturesome twin squatting three feet from the hollow in terrified bewilderment, while over him, reaching out a tentative and murderous beak, stood a stocky blue jay.

The brilliant marauder that had been winging by, ready for mischief, had seen the little shape crawl outward from the hollow, and always willing to attend to unescorted infants, had swung about and alighted silently between it and the entrance. Intending to snatch it up without a struggle, the jay was momentarily disconcerted by the instant vocal protest set up by the victim, who scrambled away toward the end of the stub. This necessitated the jay's taking a step or two forward, but before the second was completed, a small whirlwind smote the unsuspecting bird directly from the rear.

Amelia had acted with precision and dispatch. In a straight short leap she struck fairly upon the back of the amazed jay and reached forward to clutch his neck. The bird, grasping frantically with its claws, flattened itself upon the stub and whirled its head about in hurried jabbings at the determined attacker. Neither had time or breath to utter a sound, and the combat was carried on in silence. The deadly beak struck again at Amelia. She was out of reach, however, and the bird, feeling sharp teeth sinking beneath its feathers, resorted to violent struggles in the hope of throwing off that weight upon its back. It leaped upward with a discordant shriek, thrashing its wings, and the inevitable happened. Losing balance, the combatants pitched off the stub and hurtled downward in a clawing, biting tangle, leaving a mist of blue feathers in their wake.

For perhaps a dozen feet they fell, tight-locked together; then the jay's wings caught the air and in a sudden wheeling turn, it dislodged the clinging Amelia and darted away in raucous humiliation. The devoted little mother, spreading her parachute, glided safely downward, scurried back to the pine, and ascended to her thoroughly frightened offspring. Escorting it summarily into the hollow, she proceeded to assuage its fears and banish the terror of the first encounter it had experienced with the vicissitudes of the wild. An important lesson had been learned, and due to the prompt action of the mother, had been attended by no lasting detriment, the penitent youngster being perfectly willing to wait for an escort on its future excursions.

For weeks it had been hot and rainless. Amelia could not remember when the water had been so low in the lagoon, and all the long "leads," the dim cathedral aisles of the big cypress swamp, were much below their usual level. The shallow portions were quite dry, and the sphagnum moss was an unnatural brownish color that contrasted strangely with the gray-green trunks. The grass in the clearing was brittle and parched, rustling shrilly in the occasional breaths of hot and fitful breeze. The denizens of swamp and pineland felt the heat and the drought in many ways, though it brought delight to the few bears of the green gloom, who reveled in many an isolated pool swarming with fish, imprisoned in its diminishing confines.

Late one afternoon Amelia, while guarding the youngsters on the perch, caught a pungent, acrid odor on the breeze. She wrinkled her little nose and searched the wandering air currents curiously, then ran quickly to the very tip of the old pine and stared out in all directions over the woods. It was nearly dusk, and she did not see an ominous bank of murky vapor to the eastward—a billowy, purplish-black mass that rolled and wavered in huge, fantastic gropings about the obscured horizon. The breeze died down, and with it the peculiar odor; Amelia descended the trunk, and hustling her babies back into the hollow with many squeaks of injunction and command, left them and fared forth into the dusk.

Choosing to hunt upon the ground, she glided from the pine and cruised among the grasses in an absorbed, preoccupied manner. There had been no play for several evenings, the oppressive heat seeming to discourage hilarity, and a spirit of listlessness had overcome the flying-squirrel population of the woods. With her growing young to feed, however, Amelia could not afford to indulge in laziness. It was dark and warm among the grasses, and she alternately stopped and started, until a sudden whir in front appraised her of what she sought. Clinging to a swaying stem, unconscious of danger, was a large grasshopper. Now grasshoppers were fair game, and Amelia liked them well. Her night-piercing vision picked out every detail of the resting insect, perfectly motionless and not aroused by the flight of its neighbor, that had whirred away at Amelia's approach. Creeping softly forward, she bounded suddenly, like a patch of animated thistledown, fairly upon the sleeper. The green victim never knew the doom that smote it; it passed into oblivion without a struggle or a pang, and Amelia squatted in the grass and made her meal. She was as dainty in her eating as in everything else, and sitting upright, her tail curved over her back, she handled the insect in tiny forepaws, her large eyes glancing about her keenly as she ate.

Where there was one grasshopper there would be more, and Amelia knew that the big insects remained in the warm grass by night as well as day. She stalked two more before she felt satisfied, for her appetite must also suffice for two other mouths, and in her own active life she needed abundant fuel for her body. At last she finished, and mounting a convenient stump, made an elaborate toilet, smoothing her silky fur until it shone and running her paws through her whiskers until they were free of every particle of her meal. This done, she dropped to the ground and regained the pine, where she was welcomed by her eager babies.

It was very dark when she had finished her ministrations to them and she curled herself about them in a compact ball, the trio soon losing themselves in slumber. Silence reigned for half an hour. Then the little mother awoke with a start, full of an unaccountable alarm. She listened intently for a moment, her ears filled with a low murmur, a strange but insistent, far-off roar. She glanced upward, to see that the entrance of the hollow was outlined in a flickering glow that came and went with hurried, silent pulsations. A numbing dread tightening about her heart, Amelia sprang toward the opening, jostling the sleeping youngsters, who protested shrilly at her unwonted roughness.

Leaping to the perch, the squirrel gazed out at the huge, still forest that swept away from the swamp in the familiar black formation she had known so long. It was black near her tree and for some distance beyond, but another color claimed attention. Amelia looked upon a leaping, gyrating line of yellow, red, and orange light out there beyond the trees; an onrushing demon that was sweeping toward her in a devastating swath. *The forest was on fire!*

The spectacle held her spellbound, fascinated. She knew not what it was—she had never seen a flame before—but that there was something terrible in it, she realized at once. For a moment she remained immovable while that low, menacing roar grew louder. Suddenly a heavy crashing in the dry bushes and grass at the base of the pine drew her gaze downward. Her vision, piercing the gloom, showed a sight that amazed her. A big, wide-antlered buck swept outward from the trees in a magnificent bound, while in front of him, running low, were three slim does. The antler bearer stopped, whirled in his tracks as he gained the open, and stared behind him. His eyes were wild; his nostrils distended and flaring; his flanks heaving painfully as the expression of an overwhelming terror held his gaze toward the forest. He stood statuesquely for perhaps ten seconds, then wheeled and dashed madly off. No sooner had he disappeared than two rabbits darted out, flanked by a snarling, spitting wildcat, and a terror-stricken racoon. The strange quartet hurried by Amelia's tree in a formation that could have been covered by a blanket; the fear of both was in their eyes, but not from one another.

The roar grew louder; vast billows of resinous smoke poured over the grass, whipped onward by a hot wind that momentarily grew in strength. The breasts of these hurrying clouds of vapor were lit with an angry, wild glare, an ever-changing, variegated reflection of the holocaust beneath them. Faint crashes and muffled booms of falling trunks and branches drifted on the wings of the wind to where the squirrel crouched, and her momentary stupefaction passing, she whirled about and darted into the hollow.

Firmly grasping one of the silent little shapes in her mouth (for slumber had claimed them again), she emerged into the night, and hesitating not a moment, launched out into the Stygian gloom beneath the pine. Exerting every ounce of energy she swooped as far as possible, landed lightly, and ran like a flash up a tall cypress on the edge of the swamp. Leaping outward again, she sailed into the blackness ahead, her eyes glaring into every covert as she went. She instinctively knew that she must reach water, but the pools were dry.

An arm of the lagoon, reaching back into the cypresses, loomed before her. Nearly in the middle of it stood an ancient, buttressed stump some eight or ten feet high, seamed and serrated with knotholes and crevices. She saw it in an instant, and flashing up a mighty gray-green trunk along the shore of the lagoon, she ascended quickly, until the tiny twigs amid its crown trembled at her clutch. Then she swooped.

Down, down, down, she went in a rushing, gliding arc, her legs extended to the utmost, her membrane taut. She would have made it without the extra weight of the little one—just made it—but as it was, she skimmed along the surface horizontally for a few yards, lifted herself in a final sweep, and missed the stump by a foot. Instantly she struggled onward, holding her precious burden high, and in a desperate, valiant effort, gained the sanctuary. Scrambling upward, she darted around the old rampart nearly to the top, entered a yawning cavity, and laid the little one upon the solid wood at the bottom of it. Just as she disappeared, a huge, nightmarish head glided to the base of the stump and glared upward with green, malignant eyes. That tiny splash in the water a moment before had caught the attention of a denizen of the lagoon and with a sweep of a massive, plated tail, the old alligator slid over to the ripples in the still surface and stared upward expectantly.

In another moment Amelia appeared, and even in this time of stress she obeyed a prompting that was all but a part of her being. She looked before she leaped; she saw that hideous head below and gazed straight into those staring eyes. A tremor shook the devoted little mother, stark terror gripped her, even as a vision shot across her brain—a vision of a tiny, gray-furred form asleep in an old pine in the distant clearing, unconscious of that searing destruction bearing down upon it and depending upon her for life itself.

With a queer little whimper in her throat, she darted around the stump, ran down it, and leaped to a partly submerged log ten feet away. Hardly touching it, she jumped again to a floating patch of weed and then to a water-soaked branch nearby. A foaming plunge sounded behind, but she jumped again, and yet again, terrified and shaken, but indomitable. The water shallowed suddenly, another log loomed up, and in one more long leap she gained the willows that lined the shore. The drooping limbs sagged fearfully for a moment, but they held, and she was safe.

Up a cypress trunk she sped, while behind, in the muddy water, a long, dark form swung angrily about, cavernous jaws boomed together in baffled rage, and the huge reptile turned and sank downward toward the deeper reaches of the lagoon.

Amelia hurried on through the swamp and gained the clearing in a few moments. The sight that greeted her there was breathtaking; she had not realized the frightful speed of a forest fire. Even before she reached the open, she could see that just beyond was a raging furnace. Beneath her, as she swooped toward it, every sort of frantic creature rushed headlong from the devastation behind. Deer, crazed and blundering, reeled into each other and dashed madly off at wide tangents; scurrying racoons and clumsy possums scuttled through the underbrush, with glaring eyes fixed on the distant glint of water. Whole squadrons of cotton rats and rice rats, white-footed mice, and tiny shrews bunched together, or fanned out in wavering, drunken lines, some trodden on by others, some crushed by a speeding buck or wildcat. Others collapsed weakly amid the tinderlike grass, unable to take another step; slim gray foxes, wild with fear, their tongues lolling redly from narrow jaws, streaked by, never noticing.

The withering heat that marched before the conflagration seemed to shrivel all lower vegetation; cassina and scrub palmetto writhed and twisted in seeming agony; saplings bent downward and curled into weird, contorted shapes. Blazing limbs, fiery bits of bark and pinecones, dropped like a creeping barrage among the grasses, sending up spouts of living flame as their dying, burnt-out shapes ignited the fresh material they touched. Volumes of stifling smoke eddied over the ground, now high, now low, gushing outward from the roaring inferno like shadowy fingers reaching to grope for and envelop everything that lived.

Amelia, appalled and half-crazed, arrived at the edge of the clearing and stopped momentarily as the forest on the farther side seemed literally to melt with fervent heat. It seemed pure suicide to go forward into that scorching blast, but something stronger than fear impelled her dauntless little heart. She was only a tiny flying squirrel—but she was a mother.

Directly in the path of that lurid confusion was the old pine, still intact but with its scarred top smoking furiously. The nearby trees were wrapped in flames. Amelia saw the fire writhe up trunk after trunk, climb into the topmost branches like huge, glowing serpents, to fan out in the heights as a bursting, all-pervading crown of fearful red. Spouts of smoke and gushes of fire leaped upward from the ground; loud crashes came as the huge, soaring columns of burning trunks suddenly swept downward in blinding arcs of orange light.

They were all instantaneous, these impressions upon her brain. She saw the situation at a glance, for the whole clearing was as light as day; she dropped down to the crackling grasses and darted to the pine. Keeping the trunk between her and the fire, she streaked upward upon it, and even as she did so, the top burst into a halo of leaping flame. In frantic, whimpering terror she rushed in upon the youngster groveling at the bottom of the hollow, and snatching it up, turned to the entrance. A heavy tremor shook the trunk; a searing breath of the furnace outside beat in at the entrance, all but driving Amelia back in gasping agony; but as it passed she struggled outward. As she gained the stub, the old pine reeled, and a tongue of fire licked downward from the blazing top. Then, out over the grasses that crackled into nothingness below her, the squirrel swooped. A loud crash rang out behind, and the lofty shaft plunged backward into the heart of the roaring destruction, that enveloped it in a fiery embrace.

Amelia reached the trees in front in one swoop, but it took two more before she was able to breathe. The fearful heat was somewhat broken by the screening trunks, but they would last only a few minutes more. However, it was enough, and she regained the edge of the lagoon once more. Racing up a cypress, she poised among the tossing branches and shot outward over the water. But in her desperation, her brain reeling from the cataclysm that had all but engulfed her during the excitement of the last few minutes, she did not look carefully before she leaped.

As she rushed downward, her baby held firmly in her mouth while it clutched her with tiny forepaws, a sudden swirl broke the surface below her. In the midst of the disturbance, etched against the illuminated waters, appeared the head of an immense alligator, huge jaws uplifted and yellowed tusks gleaming in a livid throat. Amelia, driving straight for that living trap, was absolutely helpless; she could but continue, for there was no stopping. Her brave little heart faltered with the horror of the awaiting fate, but even in this extremity, she attempted to draw her little one closer, to shield it from those awful jaws. Her reckless courage, her unswerving devotion in the face of deadly peril, was passing for naught.

It all happened in an instant. Her plunge through space; her sighting of the doom below; her hurried clutching of her baby; then a brilliant light hurtled past her head, a strident hissing filled the air about her as a flaming brand, hurled onward by the wind, whirled by, all but scorching her in its meteoric flight. Like a darting rocket the fiery timber crashed into the water not six inches from the alligator's jaws. Green eyes, glaring with terror now, gleamed momentarily; a clashing boom sounded as the jaws closed on empty air and the massive bulk surged downward in a frantic dive, appalled by that hissing visitor from the skies.

Amelia, skimming the surface where it had disappeared, splashed lightly into the water, clambered to a bit of driftwood, and leaped to the stump. Up the furrowed wood she ran, flashed into the hollow near the top, and dropping the bewildered baby beside the other, collapsed herself, exhausted but unhurt.

About the wide lagoon that presented an impassable barrier to its consuming march, the roaring fire-demon split and wavered, circling the shore in a devastating but diminishing ring of light. Some half-hour later, when the fierce glow in the sky had sunk to a fitful glare and only scattered banners of smoke drifted across the friendly waters, three little furry heads appeared in the hollow of the old stump and stared out at the red reflection in the heavens with a restful contentment in their inscrutably liquid eyes.

* * * * *

"Amelia, the Flying Squirrel" [originally, "Assapan the Flying Squirrel"], by Alexander Sprunt Jr. Published in St. Nicholas, *December 1930. Original text owned by Joe Wheeler. Alexander Sprunt Jr. was a prolific writer of nature stories for popular magazines during the first half of the twentieth century.*

ONCE UPON A SONG

Linda Franklin with JoAnn Haase

*"If you keep a green bough within your heart,
there will come one day, to stay, a singing bird."*

—Onitsura

Her entire world had caved in on her, it seemed. Nothing, it seemed, could break her free fall into total despondency.
Until—

* * * * *

JoAnn's pain was draining the life out of her. Had it not been for her children and a certain plain brown bird, she would have missed the secret to the joy of life she discovered that warm spring evening more than twenty years ago.

I was having a hard time coping with the miserable hand life had dealt. I was abandoned, confused, discouraged. The only encouraging thought I could think was that he would surely come back and apologize to me and the kids. Then it would come clear to me, or at least I would try to understand. During those early days, with our family broken, happiness became a distant memory. Fear and anger struggled to defeat me.

I was visiting a friend one day when I realized I hadn't heard the children's voices for a while. I'm sure my face registered the panic I was feeling.

"Vickie!" I asked breathlessly, "Do you know where the kids are?"

"Yes, they are all in the park, JoAnn." She laid her hand on my arm and looked into my eyes. "The children are safe. Are you all right?"

"Just the same, I'm going to go check on them," I said, needing the reassurance that I was still a good mother after suffering yet another bout of emotional rejection.

As I neared the park, my youngest, four-year-old Freddy, burst out of the forest of saplings with his older brother and sister and Vickie's two children trailing behind him. He had something cupped in his little hands.

"Mamma, Mamma! Look what I found! I got it away from the bad dog!"

Freddy then dumped a slobbery little ball of fuzz into my hand. It was the sorriest excuse for a bird I had ever seen. The other children gathered around, and I tried to piece the story together while they all talked at once. Apparently, a neighborhood dog had destroyed a nest of chicks on a low-hanging branch; however, Freddy had managed to rescue this one. But to what end? Surely the chick would die. It was so tiny. Its eyes were barely open. Fingering its feathers, I discovered a puncture wound in his breast. There was really no hope.

I couldn't cope with another loss. I didn't want to cry anymore. If I'd had any tears left, I surely wouldn't waste them on a bird. Yet . . .

I looked past the chick into my little one's trusting eyes. Freddy was always coming to the rescue of some unfortunate creature. He was a magnet for orphans of every description. In fact, I never knew what he'd bring home next.

"You can save him, can't you, Mamma? I told 'em you could!" Freddy bragged. How could he have such confidence in me? I hadn't always been able to work miracles for him, but his trust kept encouraging me to try. Five pairs of eyes were looking at me. Five pairs of ears were listening for a word of hope. None of them were even moving, they were just . . . waiting . . . expecting. I looked back at the chick as if he held the answer. He snuggled down into my hand and blinked up at me.

I was suddenly overwhelmed with conviction: I had to try and save this helpless little chick from death. I felt my jaw set in spite of my lack of confidence. For the children's sake, I had to do my best.

I turned back toward home, the chick cradled to my breast, five youngsters trailing out behind me skipping and turning cartwheels of joy. I felt like a mother quail heading to her nest. Vickie and her children waved goodbye

as we cut our visit short in order to care for our new arrival.

There was nothing recognizable in my meager kitchen supplies that resembled bird seed, but this chick was too young to eat seed anyway. What should I feed such a tiny thing? I crumbled some whole wheat bread into a teaspoon of milk and was pleasantly surprised when the chick gobbled it down. My hands seemed much too large to feed such a tiny creature, but I was encouraged by his appetite. When he had eaten a few crumbs, I wiped his beak and placed him in the shoe box I had instructed the children to pad with a clean washcloth. Then I looked for some peroxide and sterile cotton swabs with which to clean the wound in his chest. It looked bad; pretty deep. I must have looked discouraged after I inspected and treated the wound, but little Freddy knew what to do.

With the seriousness of a minister, Freddy announced to his sister, Shauna, and older brother, Eddy Joe, "Now, we all need to pray that he will get well." We all knelt together around the little shoe box. "Dear Jesus. Thank You for sending us this little birdie. Please help him get better soon. Amen." The prayers that followed were somewhat repetitive, but there was no doubt about each child's sincerity. My faith was nonexistent, but the children were confident. The chick blinked up at his benefactors as if he felt right at home and would be well in no time.

As the children prepared for bed, I fed the chick his second meal. He snuggled into his washcloth and closed his eyes contentedly. I told the children that they should be a good example and go to sleep very quietly so as not to awaken him. Motherhood is good practice for raising a chick. Whenever I heard him rustle in the night, I fed him. He ate and went right back to sleep.

Morning came much too soon. Disgustingly bright; one of those mornings when I would have rather slept all day, but little Freddy was shaking me awake.

"His name is Tibby, Mamma," he announced.

"Tibby?" I asked, sleepily. "Who . . . ?" Slowly I realized he meant our new chick. "I've never heard that name before, Freddy. What does it mean?'

"It means he is going to get all well, Mamma," he said, nodding his head with a firmness of conviction.

When Tibby kept eating and growing for several days, I went to an auction and bought him a cage. Within a few days, he discovered the perches and even mastered the swing after a number of comical blunders. The children prayed every night. As Tibby prospered, so did my faith.

Someone told me that Tibby was a "wild canary." I hoped he would eventually display some sort of color pattern so that I could identify him more exactly, but he never developed any distinguishing marks. He was just a plain brown bird.

Before he developed his adult plumage, it was time for our family to move. I had thought, because he was maturing so rapidly, that I might be able to release him into Vickie's wilderness before we left; but Tibby was still dependent on my bread and milk formula, so he traveled with us several hundred miles to northern Canada.

Our lives now revolved around little Tibby. He became my personal icon of hope . . . a good omen, a phoenix rising from the ashes of my life. I found myself checking on him, feeling a motherly concern for him long after he could take care of himself. He was always happy to eat from my hand; grapes were his favorite, but he also enjoyed corn, fresh broccoli, and lettuce. The children checked in with him as soon as they came home from school and always asked for a report about what Tibby had been up to during their absence. Tibby was happy no matter what happened. His message came a little clearer to me every day: Why choose misery over happiness?

Tibby was, at first, an obligation. As he matured he became less and less of a burden. But when he started singing, it was I who was in his debt. Every evening as we gathered in the living room for story time and music, Tibby made his presence known. By six months of age, he was singing like the canary we had decided he must be. Although I could not find a "wild canary" listed in my bird book, his song echoed those famous singers bred specifically for song. Perhaps a pair of canaries had escaped from an aviary and tried to rear their brood out-of-doors.

It was Tibby who encouraged the children to practice their music. It was fun to play the piano with a bird singing along. In fact, Freddy sometimes practiced *more* than his hour on the piano after Tibby came to live with us. (Freddy eventually became an accomplished musician under Tibby's tutelage and today teaches music in a college.)

I really had planned to release Tibby, but now that he was several hundred miles north of his natural climate, I did not think he could survive the rigors of the Arctic. Besides, whenever I considered life without him, I felt empty inside. He stayed where I knew he would be safe: right in front of the living room window, keeping track of everything that happened. Tibby had become my confidant. When I felt no one else understood my sorrow, I found myself sharing my woes with him. His advice was always the same: "Sing and play, JoAnn!"

Tibby's songs drew me back to the piano. Except for our evening gatherings around the family Bible, I had abandoned my music. It seemed like a frivolous indulgence when my heart was so full of anguish. But Tibby's insistent cheerfulness shamed me into attempting to rise above my discouragement. If anyone had a reason to be bitter, it was he. He was in captivity. His whole family was dead. Murdered. Yet, it never seemed to occur to him that he should be unhappy. He was a gift from Eden, before joyful innocence was sacrificed to the knowledge of evil. Tibby had no sadness simply because he wouldn't accept it. There was no place in his heart to hold it. His song lifted me above the sense of uselessness that had accompanied my despair.

"Sure bad things happen," he would sing to me, leaning forward on his swing, his throat nearly bursting with joy. "But look on the sunny side; there are gardens to be planted, books to be read, songs to be sung. Life is good. Never give up. Don't worry, be happy."

Slowly my heart began to heal, and I felt my blood warming again. When I felt most reluctant to sing, when the children were gone to school and the weather was forbidding, when the darkness of my fate began to sap my energy, Tibby and I would sing and play. I would lose all track of time, abandoning my cares for a few hours in a world of complete happiness as I pounded out old hymns on my ancient piano. Our homemade harmonies lifted my fog of doubt, fear, and anger, until I could look through the rain-streaked living room window and actually see, by faith, the sun behind the clouds. My heart echoed one song in particular:

You Can Have a Song in Your Heart

You can have a melody down in your heart—
When it's aching, almost breaking;
Even though the sorrow makes the teardrops start,
You can have a melody down in your heart.

Chorus:
You can have a song in your heart in the night,

After every trial, after every mile;
Anyone can sing when the sun's shining bright,
But you need a song in your heart at night.

Do not let your worries drive your song away!
Tho' tomorrow brings its sorrow,
Just remember, after night time comes the day—
Do not let your worries drive your song away!

Soon the night will pass and morning bring the day—
I am longing for its dawning;
Until then we'll labor here and watch and pray—
Soon the night will pass and morning bring the day.
　　—E. L. Slavens and Ira Stanphill

Tibby lived with us for twelve rewarding years. He sang every day. He even sang the night before he died.

My children all have families of their own now. Yes, I helped Tibby when it might have been easier, even more sensible, not to. But today I remain forever in his debt. When that old familiar feeling of rejection overwhelms me, I have only to sit myself down at the piano, close my eyes, and listen. In that silence of soul, I can always, very clearly, as if he were right beside me, hear Tibby singing. I sit, eyes closed, in that illumination of soul that only Tibby could bring. His song, forever in my heart, was a golden chord of hope—a cord of faith let down to me from heaven. I helped him when death seemed preferable to life. I helped him—and he helped me—once upon a song.

* * * * *

"Once Upon a Song," by Linda Franklin with JoAnn Haase. Printed by permission of the authors. All rights reserved. Linda Franklin lives and writes from her home in Chetwynd, British Columbia. She has made a specialty of stories depicting the interrelationship of humans and birds.

A Waif of the Jungle

George Inness Hartley

The small monkey uttered a doleful whimper and cowered back into the pro-tecting foliage. His mother had deserted him!
And the jungle was no place for a little motherless monkey.

* * * * *

A realistic story of the daily life-and-death struggle of jungle animals. Not recommended for very small children.

* * * * *

The little fellow crouched alone. Timidly he stared about, wondering, afraid, filled with nameless dread. His wiry little fingers groped blindly for a vine, found a support, and he drew his shivering form deeper into the crotch where his mother had left him. His mother! She had been his sole companion for ten long weeks, since the day he was born; in some dim fashion he had recognized the presence of the sixteen other members of the band, but his mother had remained his only chum, the sole source of food supply, the one creature in all the world upon whom he could depend. And now she had vanished, and he was desolate and afraid.

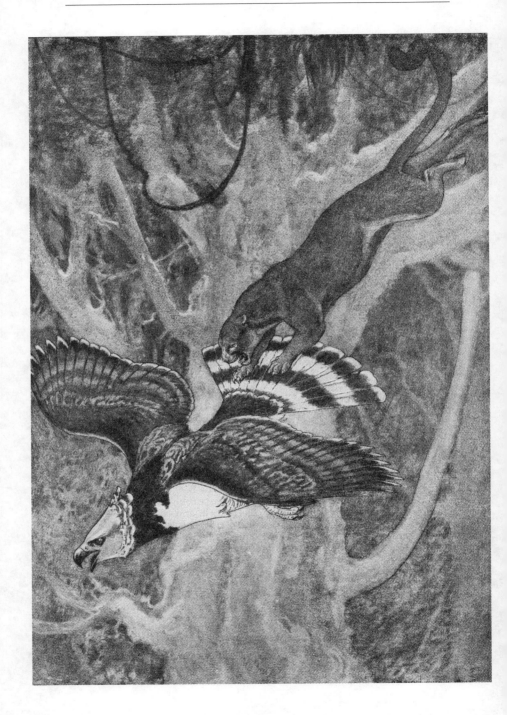

Only a short few minutes ago, she had boxed his ears until he squalled with the pain of it—in punishment for snatching at a forbidden plum. Later those same calloused hands had caressed him; soft sweet sounds had issued from her lips. He had snuggled against her, and she had tendered him a cluster of small juicy fruit. Then she had deposited him upon the broad limb close to the tree trunk, had climbed to a higher branch, and had disappeared. And with her had fled the rest of the monkey band; he had seen the swaying of branches up there, had heard the familiar crash of large bodies making swiftly off through the foliage—and she had left him behind!

The small monkey uttered a doleful whimper and cowered back even further into the protecting foliage where he had been placed. Like many of the red howlers that composed the troupe, his coat was of a brilliant auburn hue, black only upon palms of hands and feet and tail where no hair grew. But the hair of his mother had been like molten gold, brighter even than the gorgeous coat of the bearded patriarch of the band. The youngster had loved to watch the sparkling light play upon her shining body. The glittering sheen had dazzled his eyes, caused them to blink when the sun struck hardest, but he had reveled in the brightness of it all. And now the entire band had fled, even she, the most beautiful of all, and he remained an outcast, a tiny frightened atom alone in that vast mysterious jungle.

The poor little chap shivered. From the swamp beneath the mora tree in which he crouched arose the shrill snort of a tapir who had trod close to a sleeping bushmaster, that terrible reptile of the South American wilderness. Faintly he heard the rustle of a red agouti working timidly through the underbrush in search of fallen greenheart nuts. The harsh bray of a red-and-blue macaw reverberated through the forest, and long-billed toucans halted in the midst of their meal to set up an answering clank and clatter.

The listener drew a deep, apprehensive breath and whined plaintively for his parent. And from above the overhead barrier of leaves that sheltered him from the sky came his answer, that awful challenge to the jungle and all it contained, the piercing scream of a crowned harpy eagle. The heartsick waif could only retort with a shrill bleat of agony.

He remembered now. It had been a similar cry that sent the band scattering to the four winds. His solicitous mother had sallied momentarily from his side—the first time in all his life that he had known her to do so—to investigate a luscious fig cluster that dangled from a liana a few yards distant. She had been absent only a few seconds when the little fellow heard overhead the swish of an enormous pair of wings, a violent agitation of the outlying foliage, and then had come that frightful scream that stunned him so. Dimly he had heard an answering shriek of pain, the harsh, agonized cries of a monkey in desperate conflict, and then the stampede of the howler troupe off through the jungle top. He could not tell whether they were the death cries of his own mother or of some other of the band, so appalled and dazed had he been. He only knew now that he crouched there against that rough bark unattended, to face the unknown perils that surrounded him.

A faint breeze stirred the foliage. A large slate-gray feather, broken from the pinion of the eagle by contact with a twig, fluttered from a leaf, and, drifting gracefully downward, lightly tapped the overwrought creature upon the shoulder. As though it had been the touch of a ghostly finger, the little fellow gave vent to a piercing howl and, releasing his hold upon the vine, catapulted backward away from the tree trunk. Like one of the gigantic fruits which everlastingly slip crashing through the branches to bury themselves in the soft leaf mold upon the forest floor, he dove straight downward toward the ground a hundred feet below.

He fell limply, legs all astraddle, like a shapeless sawdust doll. Shackled by bonds of fright, almost unconscious, his nerveless body ripped through branch after branch that might have saved his life had he but thrust out a hand to grip the flying twigs. But he continued to drop, slowly, because of the thickness of foliage, nevertheless inertly, in a manner that would bring instant death did he strike the ground.

Fifty feet had thus been traversed before a horizontal growing vine, lashing him squarely across the shoulders, served to arouse him out of his semiconscious state. Instinctively, by a convulsive effort, his long prehensile tail, with its black leathery sole on the underside near the tip, wrapped about the tough shaggy bark. And there he swung back and forth, head downward, more dead than alive, a living pendulum marking time in the forest.

But the monkey, though only a youngster of a few months, owned all the native instincts of his tribe. Already, under the careful guidance of his mother, he had learned to negotiate the treetops with some degree of skill. He had even managed short leaps by himself, from an upper branch to a broader one lower down. From the very beginning, his tail had proved more than a fifth hand, as strong in its grasping power as the other four combined. Therefore it was with little difficulty that he presently pulled himself up until the liana came within reach of his hands. And then, though still trembling from his scare, he set off through the trees as fast as tiny hands, feet, and tail would take him.

For a quarter of an hour he traveled blindly, swiftly, with only one idea in mind—to escape the neighborhood of that horrible scream and its unearthly attendant which had touched him upon the shoulder. Presently he came to a realization that he was rushing through the trees for the first time unwatched by adoring eyes. At once courage forsook him. He threw a glance downward at the green underbrush seventy feet beneath and, shuddering at his thoughtless temerity, clung for dear life to the branch where he found himself. His little mouth puckered into a grimace of despair, and he called shakily for his mother, using a low, muffled cluck, like the distant croak of a frog. Then, regaining a mite of courage, he once more set forth, gingerly, now, though with growing confidence as he discovered that each premeditated leap did not mean a fall and that he experienced no difficulty in balancing himself upon the smallest branches.

But with waxing confidence in his own ability as a traveler, came a stronger realization of his loneliness. Hungry and forlorn and homesick, twenty times he paused to call mournfully for her who was absent, and each time he received no reply. The evening shadows began to deepen, and still he could not find her. He was lost. At last, overcome with fatigue, he crawled into a friendly tree fork all padded down with dry leaves, and, lamenting bitterly, sought solace in slumber.

The newborn sun found the tiny wayfarer much rested from his arduous journey and wholly free of that nameless fear that had dogged him throughout the previous day. Perhaps more than ever he felt the absence of his mother; in a vague way he wondered at her desertion and felt poignantly hurt by it. But the dominating idea that now filled his mind, to a belittlement of even her, was a gnawing desire for food. He felt hungry and not at all certain whence the next meal was to come. That fruit must form the basis of his diet and that the ripest fruit was to be found on the uppermost twigs, he knew; but where the proper fruit trees grew and how to reach them, experience had not yet taught him. Monkeys are not like certain carnivorous animals who, having eaten, are enabled to go several days without further sustenance. They must eat to the bursting point at least once every twenty-four hours to find life at all worth living. This youngster knew that he must find food and that quickly. Already the craving for it tortured him almost beyond endurance.

Slowly he climbed to the higher reaches of the tree in which the night had been spent. The foliage there proved barren of edible stuff. Vastly disappointed, he maneuvered with care into its next-door neighbor. Here indeed was fruit, great gleaming clusters of red berries, but alas! one mouthful proved sufficient to disillusion the hunter, and with his little red face puckered tight into a frozen grimace, much as if he had bitten into a green persimmon, he clambered disgustedly down to a lower level.

Disheartened, but rendered more desperate than ever, he worked in toward the trunk with the intention of passing on to yet another tree. As he approached the great central shaft, he noticed a spot where in some previous year a limb had rotted away, to leave a dark rent gaping in the bark. Quite without thought, following an instinctive impulse, his small paw shot into the black opening. The next instant it reappeared clasping a snow-white egg the size of a pigeon egg and much the same shape.

The finder of this strange object submitted it to a long and astonished stare. He had never seen an egg before or heard of the existence of such a thing. For a full minute, hunger forgotten, he gazed fascinated upon its gleaming surface, and then quite soberly waved it before his face, as a baby does a new plaything. He sniffed at it. A rustle among the leaves a few feet away caused him to give a nervous start; without realizing it, his fingers tightened upon the egg, and the next moment the thing was broken.

For a second or two the monkey gazed ruefully upon the fragments of his toy, then, his cravings again aroused by the delicious aroma emanating from the sticky fluid oozing through his fingers, he shot his hand into his mouth. A crow of pleasure followed the movement, and the contents of the egg vanished as though by magic.

The hunter had discovered something whose flavor far surpassed that of any fruit it had been his lot to taste, and it may be imagined that he wasted no precious seconds before delving after another such delicate morsel. With another egg balanced in his hand, he paused for a moment to gloat. For an instant he hesitated, his small lead-gray eyes glittering with anticipation. Then he thrust the shining object toward his mouth. But his chance was gone; he had waited too long. The owner of the eggs had arrived upon the scene.

Close to his head sounded a flutter of wings. A large coal-black toucan, reddish underneath and with brilliant, sulphur-colored breast, alighted upon a branch only a few inches away. The bird was almost as large as a crow and was armed with a bright green-and-black bill six inches in length, shaped like the blade of a Bowie knife. It attacked at once. The monstrous bill, serrated along its cutting edges with toothlike notches, opened and shut, and in shutting, closed upon the monkey's left ear.

There followed a squeal of pain. The egg shot from the despoiler's hand to flatten upon a branch below. The unfortunate youngster scrambled after it with one hand clasped tight about his tingling ear and the other clutching wildly at the vines in his frantic flight. The toucan remained upon its perch clanking triumphantly, master of the field. With its long, absurd tail cocked impertinently up over its back and its giant hollow bill uplifted, it jeered uproariously after him. Then as the frightened hunter vanished among the leaves, the toucan darted toward the hole that had been its home.

The monkey, still rubbing the side of his head, fled for regions where eggs did not grow. He was still hungry, nearly famished, but he no longer desired toucan eggs. He must have something else.

In walking along the bole of a thick branch, he chanced to dislodge a big section of bark, which uncovered a pair of nice large white grubs, each nearly two inches in length. These, without hesitation, he dashed into his mouth and, smacking his lips over their appetizing flavor, hurried forward. If time had permitted, he would have hunted farther for more such delightful tidbits, but his stomach cried for more filling food.

A small blue-and-green lizard scuttled before him along a branch. He snatched at the creature; but it flashed to the underside of the limb, and the untrained monkey almost lost his balance. A three-inch caterpillar, green all over, with a pair of antennalike horns, came within his reach. Like the grubs, it swiftly disappeared into his mouth, only to be instantly ejected with a guttural wail of repugnance. A second caterpillar obtained the same treatment, and thereafter the monkey passed them by without notice. He was learning fast.

In time, a tree was reached whose bark was smooth and scaly, like that of a sycamore. Small pinkish-yellow fruit flourished there in quantities, in clusters of twos and threes at the tips of the outermost twigs, and soon the jaws of the hungry one were employed at their speediest capacity. He had discovered the forest plum.

As he fed, employing two hands to maintain a constant stream of the luscious fruit toward his fast-moving jaws, a flock of yellow-headed Amazon parrots rose from the tree with a chorus of protesting screams and, circling about for a few moments, settled down beside him, shrieking, jabbering, and glaring threateningly upon him. But he was enjoying himself too much to be again driven from his food by mere birds. Many a time he had seen his mother perform on similar occasions. Parrots were old acquaintances. Therefore, casting a handful of plums aside, he raised one lordly paw and, with a majestic wave, dismissed the birds from the vicinity. And like the well-trained creatures that they were, they accepted the hint and, though still protesting shrilly, flew off.

The famished youngster stuffed himself until his little stomach bulged like a toy balloon. Then, feeling dull and sleepy, he curled up in a mass of vines near at hand that formed a convenient cradle and closed his eyes. How long he slept he did not know. His awakening proved sudden and painful. A battalion of army ants, investigating the treetops, had sent a few pioneers into the vine tangle. These without compunction applied their pincer jaws to its sleeping occupant, and the poor little chap, thus rudely aroused, left his cradle with a single bound and a yelp of pain. Among the branches he found himself further beset by the pests, and whimpering feebly, he hastened to vacate that locality.

He felt hungry again, though not with that same hollow feeling as before. The way back to the plums was barred by the ants, and to find other food, he must go farther afield. It was in a sullen frame of mind that he set out on the quest. Thoughts of his lost mother returned to him now with growing intensity. What would he not give to feel her warm body nestling against his own once more, to hear that guttural, endearing voice, and, above all, to eat the food she tendered, without thought of how the next meal was to be procured? He sighed, and, sighing, dug a small fist into his eye to keep back the tears. It was a hard thing for a little fellow of his age to be cast aside, alone in that awful place, with its biting ants and nipping toucans and sour caterpillars.

While thus mournfully reflecting, he ran full tilt into a paper nest of a family of tiny wasps, which dangled from the tip of a broad-bladed leaf directly across his path. Though small, the wasps owned enormous stings, and the wayfarer saved himself from serious damage only by a sudden drop to a lower stratum of the forest. Recovering his balance, he hastened along a liana to a point of safety, and there proceeded to fill the jungle with his groans of despair. The wasps had stung him, he had consumed too many plums, and he felt sick. He desired to die.

A large round fruit, the size and hue of a grapefruit, though in no way related to it, swished past him from the upper regions and spread its pulpy contents upon a branch farther down. The little monkey was too ill to give it heed. Upon the floor below, a large cat, dark brown as to color, with strangely short legs and a long fuzzy tail, padded softly through the forest. Coming to a partially uprooted tree whose slanting trunk stood conveniently propped against its neighbor, it sprang upward, and a moment later the sleek, sinuous body crouched behind a canopy of leaves not ten feet from the groaning youngster. There it contemplated the little fellow with evident relish. Cautiously it edged toward him, inch by inch, taking care not to disturb a leaf, its big yellow eyes fixed immovably upon its intended victim.

The monkey continued to moan his discomfort. All unseen, six feet away in the opposite direction from where lay the jaguarundi perched an enormous bird, which eyed him even more gloatingly than did the cat. The underparts of this winged giant, which stood nearly three feet tall, were pure white, with dark slate-gray feathers above, verging upon black. A tall, semicircular crest, standing like an Indian headdress, surmounted the savage head, which was armed with a great tearing bill. Tough scales covered the gigantic feet, which clutched at the branch with a throttling grip and were terrifying to look upon.

Fortune had proved kind to that harpy eagle for the past two days. Only twenty-four hours before, she had slain a full-sized monkey. Filled to stupefaction by the vast amount of meat then consumed, she had slept; and now, upon awaking, it was to discover another meal crouching before her, apparently awaiting in patience to be devoured. Fate had indeed been kind. The bird softly ruffled her feathers and edged toward her prey.

The monkey groaned piteously and then wept some more. A second fruit whirled by him, but he failed to raise his head. The harpy-eagle sidled gradually toward him—this was not the way that pirate of the air liked best to capture her meat, but, nevertheless, it would do. The jaguarundi, still hidden from the sight of both, and itself ignorant of the eagle's silent approach, crept forward. The monkey crouched with head in hands, oblivious to all but his woes. Only four feet separated him from the cat, and less than that from the eagle. The jaguarundi gathered its muscles for the spring. Its evil eyes gleamed with joyful anticipation. Then its body left the limb.

As the lank form of the cat had tautened for the plunge, an outburst of raucous laughter from that very same treetop had shattered the jungle silence. A big macaw, brilliant yellow beneath and light sky-blue above, had made a pass with its great misshapen bill at one of the big citruslike fruit that hung there. The great hook of the upper mandible drove into the tough rind; the globular fruit sweetened to overripeness by the sun, swayed under the impact and then parted from its weakened stem. Down it flew and shattered with a miniature explosion upon the branch directly before the moaning monkey.

The awakening had come in time. The jaguarundi sprang, but already its victim had vanished.

Recovering its equilibrium without difficulty, the cat glared around, amazed, its glittering orbs kindled with baffled rage. The wicked head lifted and the savage creature snarled. Its quivering body gave a sudden start. Again its muscles tightened. Less than a yard away, two other eyes, equally yellow and, if possible, even more wicked to look upon, glared straight into its own.

The long tail of the cat waved threateningly from side to side. The beast once more exposed its glistening fangs in a deep-drawn snarl. It crouched.

The eagle, caught at a disadvantage by not being in the air, sought safety in flight. Hastily she backed off a few steps. The big body darted forward and downward from the branch, and the broad wings were flung out. But this movement came too late; quick as lightning, the cat for a second time had sprung.

Down went the two marauders, a sovereign of the air, and a prince of the jungle's lower lanes, wrapped in a death grapple. High up overhead the macaw laughed again, a jibing, even more raucous laugh than before. The eagle screamed, not in defiance now, but in rage and pain. And the cat replied with a husky squall as one of the mighty talons tore through its silky skin into the soft muscles at the base of the neck.

The struggling pair crashed through the thin barrier of leaves and twigs that separated them from the ground. Owing to the thrashing of wings by the gigantic bird, the fall was broken, and they struck without bodily harm.

The dazed monkey, clinging desperately to a vine where he had been so unexpectedly hurled by the opportune bursting of the fruit became an unwilling spectator of the awful scene of conflict that now raged only a few yards beneath him. The eagle had driven the claws of her unemployed foot into the back of the cat and now, with beating wings, strove to lift her enemy back into the treetops. But the effort proved too great; the weight of the body anchored her to the ground.

From the lungs of the jaguarundi burst an agonized screech. Unable to use its jaws because of the crushing grip upon the vertebrae of its neck, the savage creature struggled fruitlessly for some moments. Then its needlelike claws dug at the bark of a fallen tree, obtained a hold, and the beast rolled upon its side. In a flash those claws had raked the feathers from the breast of its enemy.

Again the eagle screamed. Her savage beak tore at the living flesh of the cat beneath her, and her driving wings strove to pound her adversary into unconsciousness. A furry paw shot upward. There followed a scattering of feathers, and one wing hung useless. The cat uttered a triumphant snarl and, with a swift pass from the same foot, dragged the bird close to its body. Now the strong jaws obtained a hold, and sharp teeth crunched through feathers and flesh.

The eagle's piercing cry rang for the last time through the forest shades. With a final convulsive effort, her talons closed, and, meeting, set themselves in a lasting grip. The jaguarundi sobbed once and slumped back, a lifeless mass, upon the forest mold. Those dagger talons had driven deep into its spinal cord. The battle was over.

The terror-stricken spectator of this gruesome struggle clung dismally to his vine. Then as the battle drew to its tragic conclusion, he commenced dizzily to work his way upward once more. But this proved a task almost beyond his strength. His feet seemed leaden; he no longer could trust to the workings of his tail—that appendage seemed now a flaccid, nerveless thing, without strength or feeling. At last he reached the upper branches, and there found that only with difficulty could he maintain his balance. He thought he was about to die.

A violent swaying of the limb to which he clung aroused him momentarily from his lethargy. The movement continued, and he caught sight of a great form rushing straight upon him through the leaves. Then the remaining spark of strength left him. He sighed and sprawled out upon the branch. Let the end come as soon as it would; he did not care. He was tired and needed his mother. He closed his eyes.

He dimly felt himself snatched into an embrace by a pair of strong arms, his head pressed against a soft, warm body. A sweet, soothing sound, like the faint bubbling of a brook over pebbles, reached his ears. His little hands stretched feebly up to grasp a wisp of fine silken hair, and then a moist muzzle was pressed against his cheek. Then his eyes opened. He had found his mother.

* * * * *

"A Waif of the Jungle," by George Inness Hartley. Published in St. Nicholas, *March 1925. Original text owned by Joe Wheeler. George Inness Hartley of Montclair, New Jersey, was a prolific writer of nature stories and books during the first quarter of the twentieth century.*

ELSIE'S FIRST AID TO THE INJURED

Henry M. Neely

It all started with an unexpected little visitor, who explained the reason for her call with these words: "Please, sir, it's a hurted little bird."
The fee for this service? Well . . . it was simply all she had.

* * * * *

Old Doctor Potter sat in his office reading his paper and listening to the dismal patter of the rain on the windows. It was a drowsy day and he was very tired and it was not long before the paper slipped from his hands and his head fell back upon the chair.

He was not asleep. He had just fallen into that delightful doze that is half sleep and half waking, when there came a timid knocking upon the door.

The doctor sat up suddenly and collected his dignity as quickly as possible.

"Come in," he called in a deep voice.

The door did not budge.

He had almost made up his mind that he had imagined it all when the knocking came again, even more timidly than before.

"Come in," he called again, and in answer, the door was pushed slowly open, and a little girl, very thin and wet and woebegone, stuck her head into the office.

"Please, sir," she faltered. "Are you the doctor?"

Doctor Potter beamed down upon her kindly.

"Yes, little woman," he said. "What can I do for you?"

She dragged herself forward by inches until at last she was wholly within the room, and there she stood shifting from one foot to the other.

"Well, what is it?" he asked encouragingly.

"Please, sir, it's a hurted little bird," she said.

The doctor looked puzzled.

"A hurt bird," he repeated. "Have you got it with you?"

"No, sir." She pointed a wet finger toward the street. "It's out there."

Doctor Potter rose and looked out of the window.

"I don't see it," he said. "Have you got it in a cage?"

She shook her head slowly.

"No, sir," she said. "It's lyin' in th' gutter."

"In the gutter?" he repeated, growing more puzzled. Then he drew the wet little form upon his knee.

"Now tell me all about it from the beginning," he said, "and we'll see what we can do about it."

Her face brightened as though the sun had come out from behind the clouds.

"Well I wuz walkin' down th' street and it wuz rainin' awful an' I wuz runnin' an' it fell outer th' tree right into th' gutter an' it jest laid there an' cried an' it couldn't get up an' I run in here an' telled you about it an' that's about all I guess."

Doctor Potter threw back his head and laughed heartily.

"I suppose you would have exploded if you hadn't said all that in one breath, wouldn't you?" he asked. And when he saw how really serious she was, he rose and put on his hat.

"All right," he said. "Come on out and we'll see what we can do for it."

She walked confidently ahead of him as they trudged along the wet village street, and when they reached the corner she stopped suddenly and pointed to the gutter a few feet away.

"There 'tis," she said.

Doctor Potter followed the direction of her finger and saw struggling pitifully in the mud, a wounded sparrow.

"Oh, is that all it is?" he asked. "I thought it was a pet of yours."

"No," she answered. " 'Tain't a pet. It's jest a sparrer only it's hurted an' I thought you would cure it," and two big tears started down her already wet cheek.

"There, never mind," said the doctor as he picked up the wounded bird. "Come along back to my office, and we'll see what we can do for your little friend."

When they reached the steps, he turned to her and asked, "Why did you leave it lying there? Why didn't you bring it with you?"

She drew back a step.

" 'Cause I wuz 'fraid," she said. "They bites, don't they?"

"You're a little brick," he said, and led the way into the office.

She stood watching him with wondering eyes as he examined the patient, and when he muttered, "Broken leg," she seemed to understand just how serious it was.

"But you can cure it, can't you?" she asked.

He went to a drawer and took out some bandages and then to another and took out some bottles with medicine in them, and for ten minutes he worked over the little sufferer without saying a word.

When he had finished, he turned to her and said, "There, we'll let him rest here for a little while, and it won't be many days before he will be well enough to go out. What are you doing?"

She had taken something from her pocket and was examining it in her hand. She held it out to him as she answered, "It's only six cents, but I guess that will be enough, won't it? If it costs more, I guess you'll have to wait till I save more, 'cause that's all I've got."

He thought for a long time before he answered.

"Well, I'll tell you," he said finally. "You keep that money until I get ready to make out my bill, and when I am ready to do that, I'll let you know. That's the way we always do business. Meanwhile, we'll put your sick friend in the box of soft cotton where he can rest easily. And now you must tell me your name and address so that I will know where to send my bill."

She watched him write on a card,

ELSIE RITTER
147 Main St.
(Bird with broken leg)

and then she said Goodbye to him very seriously, as any of his patients would have done, and went out.

A week went by and then another, but still she did not get the bill and she was going to call on him and remind him of it when one day she received a box and a letter in the mail. When she opened the box, she gave a little cry of surprise and delight and drew out to the astonished sight of her mother, a beautiful bronze medal tied with ribbon and arranged with a pin to fasten it to her dress.

But even the wonder that she felt at seeing her name engraved upon one side of the medal did not equal her wonder at the letter that accompanied it. It said,

MY DEAR LITTLE GIRL,

Have you ever heard of the Society for the Prevention of Cruelty to Animals? You probably have not, but at one of our meetings the other day, Doctor Potter, who is our Treasurer, told us the story of a kind-hearted little girl who had run through the rain to get him to help a suffering bird which she was afraid to touch and of how that little girl had offered to give him all her pennies if he would cure it. We were all very much interested in the story. Our Society gives out Medals of Honor every year to whomever we think worthy of them, and when Doctor Potter said he thought that little girl deserved one, we all agreed that she did. If you do not understand it all, just ask your mother to explain it to you.

With the very best wishes, I am

Your friend and admirer,
JAMES H. ROBERTS
(Corresponding Secretary)

* * * * *

"Elsie's First Aid to the Injured," by Henry M. Neely. Published in St. Nicholas, *September 1906. Original text owned by Joe Wheeler. Henry M. Neely wrote for turn-of-the-twentieth century popular magazines.*

THE DARNING NEEDLE

Author Unknown

In our throwaway society, who today takes the time to darn holes in socks and other clothes? Virtually nobody. But in earlier days, money was usually scarce, so most every household contained darning needles. Certainly this story's 1880 reading audience would have fully understood the tie-in to the ferocious tiger of the insect world: the dragonfly.

* * * * *

As you see by the picture, it is not the one-eyed "stocking doctor" that we are about to introduce you to. No, indeed; our aristocratic little acquaintance would own no connection with that unpretending but very useful member of society. And yet we are suspicious that our little aristocrat of the most wonderful vision, unsurpassed nimbleness, and worldwide acquaintance is, after all, a sort of namesake of the stiff needle, whose only eye is "put out," and whose whole knowledge of the world is confined to the narrow limits of the stocking basket.

My darning needle has the wise family name *Libellulidae*, the plain English of which is "dragonfly." It doesn't object to either of these names, or even to the common name of "darning needle," if you only don't associate it with anything stiff or blind. It is really no clumsy affair. There is not a stiff joint in its body, and as for seeing things, why, bless your eyes! It is a perfect marvel. You never saw anything more wonderful. It would take your bright-eyed, smart little Johnny six hours—the longest, busiest hours he ever spent in his life—just to count the eyes of the dragonfly. Twenty-four thousand eyes! Just think of a little chap with twelve thousand eyes to your one. He can look to the right and to the left, down and up, backward and forward, toward all points of the compass at the same instant of time. Who can tell all that he sees? Wouldn't you like to borrow his eyes for about ten minutes?

The dragonfly is not only marvelous on account of its vast number of eyes, but it is curious in many ways. There are about two hundred known species, some of which are very beautiful. The largest and most brilliant kinds are found on the Amazon River. "Some of them," says a traveler, "with green or crimson bodies seven inches long, and their elegant, lacelike wings tipped with white or yellow."

The dragonfly is the most ferocious of all insects, and he has for this reason been called the "devil's darning needle," but it is better to drop the big adjective and not call hard names. Yet he is truly the greatest cannibal of the insect world. He dines with keenest relish upon his many cousins, has a special appetite for tender young mosquitoes, and does not hesitate to devour the prettiest, loveliest butterflies or any of the family relatives that he is able to catch.

All the little fellows are afraid of him, but it is useless to try to escape him. Even the swift mosquito, with its three thousand vibrations of the wing a minute, cannot outfly this terrible, swift dragon.

He takes his meals while on the wing—a whole insect at one swallow—and you can hardly guess how many victims are served up for a good "square meal." Quite a little swarm is needed for his dinner, and he is always ready to make way with all the scattering ones that he finds for lunch between meals.

The dragonfly knows all the ways of the world. He can dart backward just as well as forward, and fly sideways just as well as any other way, and so there is no chance to get out of his way. When he once goes for his victim, it is all over with it.

Naturalists have been greatly interested in this insect and have studied its habits closely from its babyhood up.

Mrs. Dragon is a firm believer in the use of plenty of water in bringing up her babies, so all her little ones begin life in an aquatic nursery. From a leaf of

a water plant, in which they are at first cuddled up, they come out with rough-looking, grublike bodies, having six sprawling legs. They find themselves all alone in the world. Their mother has gone and left them, and they have no one to provide them with their bread and dinner. They must stir themselves and grub it for a living. But they have such a stupid, lubber-heel look, that no one would think they knew enough to take care of themselves. On their head is something that looks like a hood, and this is drawn over their faces as though they were ashamed.

But this hood is only their natural headdress. These little water nymphs don't really wear their hoods for bonnets to keep them from taking cold, but they are really masks, and very curious ones too. This mask is made of hinges, slides, and hooks; and it is their trap to get a living. When they see something that they would relish for dinner, the hinges spring open, the slides shove out, and the hooks cling in, and in one instant of time their prey is secured. And that is the way these dumpish-looking little chaps "go a-fishing." You surely would never call them dull fellows if you should once see the lively way they serve up refreshments. Quicker than we can tell it, they pack their lunch baskets from capsized gnat and mosquito boats, and they overtake the swift little tadpoles and serve them up in "smacking good" meat pies.

Perhaps you would like to know how these little fellows get about so fast. Neither fins nor paddles of any kind are used in chasing their prey, nor to help them handle it when caught. But to get about they have a way of their own, and, a few years ago, a British war vessel was built to go by a method like theirs.

You may have read that Benjamin Franklin once had an idea that a boat could be made with a pump in the stern, by which water could be drawn in and pumped out with such force as to propel the boat along. But the ingenious Franklin, although he could coax lightning from the clouds and make it obey him, had to give up the idea of pumping boats about. And here is just where this little grub beats the great philosopher. In the stern of his little worm-skin boat, he has a pump that works like a charm. When the little nymph wants to go on an exploring voyage, his clever little muscles instantly set the pump at work, and away shoots the boat like a rocket, while at the prow of the boat is the masked pirate, always ready for his booty. He is voracious and banquets on multitudes of little creatures during the one year of his grub life.

At the end of the year, the little pump-boat that has served him so well is anchored to a water plant, and in two hours Jack, the sailor-grub, starts out on another voyage.

But this is an aerial trip. He hoists sail, unfolding four lovely wings of gauze, and speeds away into the air, the rich-robed monarch of the insect world.

To every enemy of insects, the dragonfly is a friend, for what uncounted hosts of water insects does the swift boat of this pirate overtake before it comes to shore, and what swarms and swarms of little animal life have been buried in that one grave—the voracious, never-satisfied, long stomach of the great insect dragon!

But only insects have reason to fear him; and he generally proves quite sociable with the boys and girls who cross his path, knowing himself well insured against capture by his swift-darting wings and myriad eyes. You will find him much more difficult to catch than his cousin butterfly, but when you go fishing, he will flit along the bank in front of you as you wade through marshy places, or hover above the tangle of driftwood near which you have dropped your line, as if he enjoyed your company. Now and then, perhaps, he will even poise gracefully for a moment above your outstretched rod, or silently settle on the very same log on which you are seated, and almost within reach of your hand. Make the slightest motion to entrap him, and see how quickly he is gone! Yet he does not go far, returning sometimes to the very spot from which you drove him away. Be sure, then, that at least some hundreds of his thousands of eyes are on you; but, though he is such a terror to his own tribe and kindred, he is at peace with all mankind, and you may become acquainted with this beautiful but fierce darning needle with as much safety as with the homely, stupid one in grandmother's stocking basket.

* * * * *

"The Darning Needle," author unknown. Published in St. Nicholas, *August 1880. Original text owned by Joe Wheeler.*

A Story About Ancestors

Dorothy Canfield Fisher

*Ostensibly this is a story about a grandfather—and little black and white
animals that are known everywhere for their terrible stench.*
As I said: ostensibly this is what this story is all about.

* * * * *

Jimmy came to the door of the living room and stopped short, looking
very cross to see that his mother had a caller. He didn't look as cross as his
mother felt, for the caller was an old gentleman whom she had never seen
before, who said he was a distant cousin, and who wanted to find out all
about their great-grandfathers. He seemed to think they were very important, but Jimmy's mother didn't, and she was wishing very much he would
go away and ask somebody else. Jimmy wished so, too, from the expression
on his face.

Then he went away, and his mother heard the typewriter in her study tap-
ping slowly. When he came back, he went into the room, endured being introduced to the old gentleman, and did not squirm too visibly when the
caller said that the shape of his head was like that of one of his great uncles'.
He had a piece of paper in his hand, and as soon as he could, he laid it on his
mother's lap and looked at her hopefully. On it he had written:

Dear Mother

Will you please tell me a made-to-order story about an ironing-board, a big grandfather clock, a bag of popcorn, a bottle of ink, a yellow and black and red stone.

Goodbye Mother

From Jimmy

His mother read it and raised her eyebrows. Jimmy looked at the old gentleman and sighed. It was plain he wished he could do something more than sigh. So did his mother.

"A fine little chap," said the gentleman.

Jimmy shuddered and went away.

But not far. For at the very instant when the old gentleman was saying Goodbye at the door, Jimmy's mother felt herself clutched from behind.

"Now!" said Jimmy. "Let's beat it."

So they did, off into the pinewoods, where they couldn't be seen by any more callers.

But still they couldn't seem to get rid of the old gentleman's ideas. Perhaps they had slipped into the story when Jimmy had laid the paper on his mother's lap.

"It's funny," she said, "and you may not like it very well; but this very story is about your great-grandfather and your grandfather."

Jimmy looked alarmed.

"But there's a skunk in it," said his mother.

"Oh, that's all right then," said Jimmy. "Go ahead."

"It began rather a long time ago, maybe forty-five years ago, when my grandfather (that's your great-grandfather) was asked to make an address before a big meeting of teachers down in Massachusetts. He was a very careful man who believed in getting everything ready beforehand, and he started in at once to make ready for this. He had his best suit cleaned, bought himself a fresh necktie, wrote his speech all out, then copied it; more than a week before the departure day, he had spoken to the livery-stable man about driving him to the train. For there weren't many trains a day, forty-five years ago, and to get to his meeting on time, he'd have to be driven fifteen miles to a junction where he could catch a train going south.

"The morning in September when he was to start was lovely and sunny.

His necktie looked splendid when tied, and his coffee was just as he liked it. But right there his good luck stopped, for when he went into his study to get his clean-copied speech, he saw something dreadful. He had left the sheets all spread around, so the ink would dry well, and to hold them down, he had put on them a large oval paperweight of onyx which somebody had brought him as a present from the Holy Land—the way they do to ministers."

"What's onyx?" asked Jimmy.

"It's a shiny sort of stone, red and yellow and black, that's used for paperweights," said his mother.

"Oh, yes," said Jimmy. "Teacher has one on her desk. I didn't know what its name was. What was the matter with this one?"

"Matter enough. The cat had been playing with it and had tipped it over against the ink-bottle, and had knocked it over. And all night long the spilled ink had been soaking into the nice clean, freshly copied pages of Grandfather's speech!

"It was too late to do anything about it, for Patrick, the livery-stable man, had just driven up to the door. There wasn't even time to say anything about it, although Grandfather had plenty he could have said. He just ground his teeth together hard, crammed his hat on over his eyes, and snatched up the rough notes for his speech. They were rather scribbly and written crisscross of the paper, and he hadn't wanted to try to read them before an audience; but there wasn't anything else he could do now. He was lucky, in fact, that he had happened to put them on a shelf, and not on the table with his clean copy.

"He felt a little better after an hour's driving, for two reasons. For one, the livery-stable man was rather fresh from Ireland and had a lovely brogue that tickled Grandfather to hear, and he called Grandfather 'Your Reverence,' just like somebody in a story. And then he had turned out with his best outfit, the fast team of trotters, and his elegant new light wagon, the finest in town, with tan-colored velvet cushions and bright red wheels. Grandfather never cared anything about putting on style, but he always liked a good horse, and he did enjoy dusting along the road after those two sorrel spankers, heads up, tails flying, hoofs beating time together like a drummer rattling out a double-quick tattoo. Patrick was proud of them, and every time they went through a village he'd brisk his pair up to their fastest trot. Then he and Grandfather would put their heads together and pretend to be talking and not thinking a thing about their fast horses, although, as a matter of fact, they were very much put out if people didn't turn their heads to look after them as they rushed through.

"In between villages, where there wasn't anybody to see them, they often let the horses walk, and as they began to go downhill into Ransom's ravine, Patrick put the brake on and looked ahead sharply. The road was very rough and stony there, and, after dipping down steeply, reached a narrow bridge across a deep, black, crack in the rocks, with a little mountain stream rushing and shouting at the bottom. It was something like a canyon in your geography book, only not so wide and deep. Plenty deep enough, though, for all drivers to want to keep their wits about them when they crossed the bridge.

"They were still a good way from it, when they made out something black and white ahead of them, just going onto the bridge.

" 'That can't be a—' said Patrick, shading his eyes with his hand, for the bushes were thick on each side of the road just there, and the road was in shadow.

" 'Yes, it is, too,' said Grandfather, putting his hand out on the reins in a hurry. 'Don't you go a step nearer till he gets out of the way.'

"Patrick was just as ready to stop as anybody. He hadn't been in America very long, but plenty long enough to learn a good deal about skunks.

" 'Aren't they bold!' said Grandfather, surprised to see one right in the middle of the road.

" 'There isn't a thing for them to fear,' said Patrick, bitterly.

" 'Look—there's another, just coming out of the bushes,' said Grandfather.

" 'Two more,' said Patrick, standing up in the wagon, to see better. 'A family of them, Your Reverence,' he went on, sitting down hard.

"Sure enough, it was a mother skunk with five young ones, half-grown, about as big as sizable kittens. And they were surely out for a good time. The mother lay down spang in the middle of the road in the soft dust and spread out her legs comfortably, while the young ones began to play, frolicking up and down the bridge and jumping at each other in and out of the bushes.

"Grandfather looked at Patrick. And Patrick looked at Grandfather. Then Grandfather looked at his watch.

" 'Is there any way around?' he asked.

" 'No, Your Reverence, not unless you go back ten miles to Bowley's crossroads. This is the only bridge over the ravine between here and Pentonsville.'

" 'You don't say so!' said Grandfather, rather put out with Patrick.

"They waited a minute or two. Then Grandfather said: 'Come, come, this will never do! Let's drive up nearer and throw stones at them.'

" 'Never in this world,' said Patrick. 'My wagon cost me seventy-five dollars, and it's not a nickel it would be worth if we got the creatures' bad feelings stirred up. In fact, we're a little too near right now to please me.'

" 'Well,' said Grandfather, 'I'll hold the horses. You go along on foot and throw stones.'

" 'Saving your presence,' said Patrick, 'I had a brother once threw a stone at a skunk. One is enough for one family.'

" 'Nonsense!' said Grandfather. 'It would be perfectly safe from as far as you could throw a stone. Go along with you.'

" 'You never came near my poor brother right after he did it,' said Patrick. 'But, if you like, I'll hold the horses, and you can try it yourself.'

"Now Grandfather could throw a stone as far as the next man, and he didn't really believe that he would come to any harm. But all the same, it would be pretty serious if he did. He had often caught the scent of skunk from half a mile away, and it scared him to think what it might be like close up. Besides, it wouldn't have to be very bad, to be plenty bad enough to keep him from making his speech. He had a picture of himself standing up on the platform, with ever so slight an odor of skunk floating out from him over the audience. And he knew it wouldn't do.

" 'No, we'll wait a while,' he said to Patrick. 'She can't stay there much longer.'

"But she did. The spot just suited her, so soft and quiet, and with plenty of hide-and-seek places for children. You could see how she was enjoying it. She stretched out one leg and then another, turned over, rolled, sat up and scratched, and then started in to wash herself from head to foot, just like a cat in front of the kitchen stove.

"Grandfather and Patrick gave a groan. And Patrick just gave up. It was plain to see that he couldn't think of anything to do but sit there and wait. Grandfather didn't believe in giving up, ever. So he cast around in his mind and hit on an idea.

" 'Maybe we can scare them away by yelling and shouting,' he suggested.

" 'Maybe,' said Patrick, looking uneasy. 'But don't you yell a yell, Your Reverence, till I get my team farther away. The very harness would be no good to me if anything should happen.'

"He backed the horses up the road a little and then said, 'Well, we might try it. But not very loud if you please, sir. It might not be to her taste.'

" 'It wouldn't be any use unless it was loud,' said Grandfather.

" 'It's not your wagon,' said Patrick, getting angry.

" 'It's my best suit of clothes,' said Grandfather, angry himself, 'and you have promised to get me to the junction in time for that train.'

" 'Well, here goes,' said Patrick, and he said in rather a loudish voice, 'Get off wid ye! Whey! Whey!' the way you'd talk to a cow in the cabbages.

" 'Oh, you'll never get anywhere with that sort of business!' said Grandfather, crossly. He stood up in the wagon to get the good of his lungs and drew a deep breath and began to yell like an Indian or a stuck pig, at the top of his voice. He was noted for the loudness of his voice too. They used to come from all around to get him to address open-air meetings, because he could be heard from so far. He was very cross indeed, by this time, and he let himself go, whooping and howling and bellowing till he was black in the face. He noticed after a while that Patrick wasn't helping any, and glanced down to see why. There was Patrick, doubled over the arm of the seat, nearly dead with laughing.

"Grandfather stopped yelling and looked at Patrick coldly. Patrick was ashamed of himself, but he couldn't stop.

" 'I can't help it, Your Reverence,' he said, giggling and wiping his eyes. 'It's like as if you were making a speech to the beasts, or preaching them a sermon, and they listening as pleased as any old woman in her pew.'

"As a matter of fact, the skunks hadn't objected at all to Grandfather's noise. The mother had turned her head toward him, and two of the young ones had stopped playing, but they showed no signs of thinking his hullabaloo disagreeable. Somebody told Grandfather afterward that skunks are often quite deaf.

"Grandfather was so angry with Patrick and with the skunks and with himself by this time, that I'm sure I don't know what would have happened if at that very minute they hadn't seen, far away on the other side of the skunks, a pair of horses come into sight where the road goes over the brow of the hill. Behind the horses was a lumber wagon, with a canvas cover thrown over some bulky-looking objects. But the load couldn't have been heavy, for the horses came along at a good trot. They did, that is, till they came near enough to see the black-and-white animals playing around in the road. Then the driver stopped so short that the wagon almost shoved the horses off their feet from behind.

"Patrick burst out laughing again, and this time Grandfather laughed with him. Not a good loud ha! ha! for he was still hot and angry, but a little grunt of a laugh he couldn't keep back. They saw the driver and a little boy in the seat of the lumber wagon peering down the road, shading their eyes with their hands.

" 'Are those skunks?' shouted the man to Grandfather and Patrick. He was so far away that they could only just catch what he said, although he was evidently yelling as loud as he could.

" 'And what else?' yelled Patrick back at him.

"The man stared at the animals harder for a moment, as if to be sure, and then yelled, 'Why don't you do something about it?'

" 'Well, the nerve of him!' said Patrick and Grandfather, so mad at the man they forgot to be mad at each other.

" 'Do it yourself!' shouted Patrick.

" 'Do what?' asked the man.

" 'For goodness' sake!' said Grandfather, too exasperated to live. Then he raised his voice and shouted, 'Throw some stones at them!'

" 'I dassent,' yelled back the man. 'Got some vallyble antiques in my wagon.'

" 'Get out on foot and throw stones,' shouted Patrick.

" 'Not on your life!' yelled the man.

" 'Some people are too selfish for this world!' said Patrick to Grandfather indignantly. He turned his back, as far as he could, on the skunks and the lumber wagon and the man and the boy, and lighted his little short pipe. 'We'll just be waiting,' he said to Grandfather, 'for there's nothing else to do.'

"So they waited. Grandfather held his watch in his hand, watching the second hand going around faster and faster. The horses stamped and switched their tails against the flies, and tossed their heads till Patrick got out and undid the checkreins.

"Over in the lumber wagon, Grandfather could see the little boy talking and talking to the man, and he wondered what the child could find to say that took so long. By and by, he saw the little boy get out of the wagon and disappear in the bushes; and a few minutes later, to their great astonishment, he came out of the woods beside the road where Grandfather and Patrick sat waiting.

" 'How'd you get here?' they asked. 'Is there another bridge over the ravine?'

" 'No, but there's a narrow place where the rocks come pretty close together, and a tree's fallen across,' he told them. 'I had an idea, and it was too far away to yell at you, so I came around to tell you.'

" 'Well, what's your idea?' asked Grandfather, thinking it couldn't amount to much.

"The little boy began. 'Old Judge Pellsew is going to move out West, to live with his married daughter, and before he left he asked my father to take some of his old family relics up to his niece's house in Arlington, and that's where we are going. It's mostly a grandfather's clock, and a few chairs.'

" 'Well,' said Grandfather, very short, 'I don't see what that's got to do with me. I must be at the junction in time for the eleven-forty-five train south.'

" 'We live at the junction,' said the little boy, 'so how would this do? We'll carry the things out into the woods, up the ravine, to the narrow place where I crossed, and you come there to help us get them across and load them into your wagon. Then your team can turn around and carry the antiques back to Arlington, and we'll turn around and carry you back to the junction.'

" 'I don't see myself,' said Grandfather, who must have been sixty years old then, 'I don't see myself carrying one end of a grandfather's clock and walking along a fallen tree over a thirty-foot drop.'

" 'Oh, that'll be all right,' said the little boy. 'One of the things we have is an ironing board, an extra long one, and we can lay that down for a bridge. Then the last fellow across can pull it over and take it along.'

" 'It might be worth trying,' said Grandfather, doubtfully.

"The little boy put his hands up to his mouth and yelled to his father, ' 'S all right!' and they saw the man get out of the wagon at once and begin to unload the things from the back.

"Patrick tied his horses, and they hurried off into the woods after the little boy, for they hadn't a minute to lose. The man was already at the narrow place with the ironing board and two of the chairs. He laid down the board and it was just long enough. The little boy had to steady it with his foot as Patrick ran across it and grabbed the two chairs. Then the man rushed back to his wagon and brought the clock along, Grandfather helping carry it across the board. They got it into Patrick's wagon and set it up in the front seat, and tied it in with the hitch ropes. They then all tore back to the narrow place and skipped across the ironing board, all but Patrick, who stooped over to pick it up. But the ironing board was heavier than he thought and slipped right out of his hands and went falling down and down into the ravine. Patrick looked scared, but the man called to him, 'Never mind! 'Twa'n't one of the antiques!' And then as Patrick nodded, relieved, he added, still shouting over his shoulder as he ran, 'The things are to go to Mrs. Pettingill's, on the West Road.'

" 'I have a brother living on the next farm to there,' Patrick shouted back. 'They'll get there all right.'

"Grandfather and the man and the little boy piled into the empty lumber wagon, the horses were turned around double-quick, and off they started, lickety-split. Grandfather knew they never could make it. But the man wanted to show that Patrick wasn't the only person to have fast horses, and he kept his on the run for most of the four miles to the junction.

"At that, they'd have missed the train if it hadn't been a little late. They saw it pulling into the station as they came around the turn into the village street, and the man let out a yell at his horses. Down the slope they came, slam-banging along, Grandfather holding to his hat with one hand and to the side of the seat with the other. The conductor of the train thought it was a runaway, and stopped to see what would happen. And that was what saved Grandfather. They slued up in front of the station, the horses lathering white, the wagon swinging over on two wheels, and Grandfather fell out, shouting, 'Hold on! Hold on! Just a minute!' I tell you he could hardly believe it when he actually found himself sitting in the train, taking out his pocketbook, just like any other passenger, to pay for his ticket."

"He must have been feeling just about all right!" commented Jimmy, and rolled over from where he lay on the pine needles.

His mother looked at him hard and shook her head. Jimmy sat up quickly.

"Great Scott, Mother, it wasn't the wrong train!"

"No, there was but one southbound train a day in those days. No, it was the right train all right. But halfway there, he remembered that he had left the notes for his speech in Patrick's wagon when he had made the change."

"For the land of—" Jimmy was horrified. "What did he do?"

"He didn't know what to do. And the closer he got to North Adams, the less he knew. He had been asked to tell them something about universities in England, and he had looked up lots of dates and history and statistics and things, but he couldn't possibly remember them out of his head. What's more, he was so shaken up that he couldn't seem to think even what the main part of his speech was about! Indeed, when he stood upon the platform and faced his audience, he hadn't thought of a single word to say."

Jimmy looked miserably worried. He'd forgotten the whole middle part of his recitation the last time there was an entertainment at school. So he knew what it was like. He swallowed, in sympathy. "Well—"

"Here is what he did. It came to him, as he looked around the crowd and saw how friendly they seemed. He just started in at the beginning and told them all about what had happened—about the kitten that played with the paperweight, and his driving so far to get his train, and the skunks and his yelling at them, and what he said, and what Patrick said. He had intended it only as an explanation of why he hadn't his speech ready. But do you know the audience seemed to think there was something funny about it! They got into such gales of laughing that he had to stop two or three times. And when he came to the last part, where he scrambled onto the train, they all broke out applauding as if it were the end of a race.

"By that time Grandfather had his nerve back again, and when he told them about leaving his notes, he went on, 'So I haven't any speech at all to make. But see here, maybe we can make one together. You must have wanted to know about English universities or you wouldn't have asked me to talk about them. Suppose you ask me what it was you wanted to know, and I'll answer your questions?'

"And what do you think! It was the greatest success. Everybody was sort of stirred up about the skunks and thus weren't afraid to ask questions. And what they asked made Grandfather think of the things he had planned to say, and they had a lovely time. Grandfather used to say that he'd never spent a better hour with an audience."

"I suppose he could use his notes for another time too," said Jimmy, lying down again.

"No, he never could find them. When he went back, he asked Patrick about them, of course, but they hadn't been seen. Patrick thought they'd fallen out on the way back. Grandfather put a notice in the newspaper and offered a reward, but nobody ever paid any attention to it."

Jimmy's mother tried to make this sound like the end, but Jimmy cornered her by asking, "Didn't anybody ever find them?"

"Well, yes," she said, "although that part doesn't really belong in here. It was strange! Years went by, and Grandfather grew to be an old, old man, who didn't make speeches anymore. Then it was his son, my father, your grandfather, who gave the lectures. And one autumn, about twenty-five years after this, he was asked to speak to the Massachusetts teachers. There wasn't anything unusual about this, for they meet every year and always have to have people lecture them. But while he was still wondering what to talk about, little Alta Brown came up on the front porch with some old yellow papers in her hand. 'Grandmother says to tell you she thinks these must belong to you,' she said to your grandfather. 'She had a clock-mender tinker up the grandfather's clock yesterday, and he found these in under a sort of false bottom. Grandmother thought it looked like your handwriting.'

"And there were the notes, for Alta's grandmother was the Mrs. Pettingill to whom the old clock had gone. Somehow they'd been slipped into the clock when it was put in Patrick's wagon. Maybe the man put them there to make sure they didn't blow out and forgot to say anything about it. Grandfather never thought of asking him. In fact, he didn't know his name and never saw him before or after that day.

"Well, my father was a great joker, and he thought, just for fun, he would tell the audience down in North Adams the story of the speech and then read it to them, twenty-five years behind-time. He thought perhaps it would amuse them. And it did. He happened to speak in the very same hall where Grandfather had been, and the second audience laughed jut as hard over those skunks as the first one had. As he talked, an idea came to Father, and when he finished he said, 'It is quite possible that, among the older people here today, there may be someone who was present twenty-five years ago. It would be very interesting if so.'

"Then he stopped, and everybody in the audience turned his head around to see if anybody stood up. Father had half expected to see one or two old, old men stand up. But nobody did. Twenty-five years is a long time, after all.

"But right behind him, on the platform, he now heard somebody laughing, and, turning around, saw that it was the young mayor of the city, who was up there to give an address of welcome. He didn't look more than forty years old, and couldn't possibly have been a teacher twenty-five years before that. But he now stood up and came forward to the front of the platform. 'I wasn't *here,* on that occasion,' he said, while everybody held his breath to hear what he could possibly have to say. 'But I was *there.* I was the little boy who had the idea of using the ironing board as a bridge.'

"At this, everybody began to laugh again, and some people clapped their hands. But he waved his arms to show them that he hadn't finished, and went on: 'And now I'm going to tell you something which I have never divulged to a soul from that day to this. But before I do, I wish to express a hope that there are plenty of baseball fans in this audience, people who really appreciate the high importance of baseball.'

"Everybody stared. What in the world had baseball to do with that story?

" 'Our town team was going to play the last game of the season that day, and

I was crazy to go. But my father was an old-fashioned farmer who thought that games were all foolishness. So when he said I had to go up to Arlington with him to help load and unload those darned old antiques, I didn't even dare ask to stay to go to the baseball game. I felt pretty sore and mad about it, you can imagine, and more and more so as our horses trotted along, faster and faster, carrying me farther and farther from the baseball field. Although I knew there wasn't the least hope, I kept on hoping, as children will, that something would happen—an earthquake, a flood, or one of the horses dropping dead with heart failure. But although I knew all about them and had often played with them when I was visiting the Penrose boys, I never once dreamed that that family of black-and-white cats on the Penrose farm could possibly be of any use in—'

"But he never got any further. The very minute he said the word 'cats,' somebody in the audience snorted and shouted out a great 'Haw! Haw!' And then, like forty thousand bunches of firecrackers going off at once, everybody saw what had happened and burst out, just screaming with laughing. The more they laughed, the more they saw how funny it had been, and that made them laugh harder.

"My father laughed the hardest of all. He used to say afterward that they had to laugh twenty-five years' worth, all at once, to make up for the twenty-five years the joke had been kept dark."

* * * * *

Jimmy and his mother got up and strolled back through the orchard toward the house, Jimmy thinking over the story silently, as he likes to do when there has been a good deal in it. Finally, "You didn't say anything about the bag of popcorn," he said. "But I suppose he bought that and ate it on the train, going down."

"Yes," said his mother, "I suppose that was where the popcorn came in."

* * * * *

"A Story About Ancestors," by Dorothy Canfield Fisher. Published in St. Nicholas, *February 1925. Original text owned by Joe Wheeler. Dorothy Canfield Fisher (1879–1958) wrote mainly from Arlington, Vermont. She wrote more than forty books, including novels, short story collections, juvenile works, and non-fiction. She is considered to be one of the leading writers of her time. Among her books are* The Squirrel Cage, The Bent Twig, *and* The Home-Maker.

HANGING ON

P. J. Platz

Huey was only a sparrow, and it seemed ridiculous to try and save it, but somehow Charlotte felt saving Huey was supremely important. That her seven-year marriage with Daniel was crumbling around her only made the bickering over the bird surreal.

* * * * *

The battered blue pickup thundered away down the drive, trailing a cloud of summer dust. Charlotte watched it go from her seat on the front porch, her brown eyes steady and quiet. One more trip, she thought, and Daniel would have separated all the His from the Hers and hauled it into his new apartment in town.

This dividing of the goods was an ugly business. Ending a marriage was such an abstract thing, until you watched a truckload of furniture disappearing down the drive. That made it real. She wondered if the house would feel different tonight without Daniel in it.

Their seven years together was ending quietly, just as it had begun, and in a way, that seemed appropriate. She and Daniel had always been quiet people.

That was probably part of the problem. They should have talked more, *communicated* more. That's what all the talk shows and advice books said—talk it out, tough it out, make it work, hang on. But Charlotte knew that the harder you held something, the more it struggled to get away.

Sometimes you just had to let go. Like with Huey.

She looked down at the old cardboard box on the floor at her feet. A fledgling sparrow was perched on the edge, its head cocked, one bright black eye watching her curiously. "Hello, Huey." She extended her hand, and the bird hopped up into her palm.

They'd found him three weeks ago on the floor of the old barn they used as a garage, a squawking bundle of naked, wrinkled pink that had tumbled from a nest high in the peak of the roof. "Stupid, ugly things," Daniel had grumbled, sweeping it aside with the broom. He'd been angry that morning, but Charlotte couldn't remember why. All she could remember was looking down at the pathetic flopping thing that Daniel had swept into the corner like another piece of litter.

"It'll die there," she'd told him, and he'd mumbled some panacea about things that were meant to be. And maybe he'd been right about that; maybe that particular sparrow was one of the vast number slated to lose nature's lottery in its first year; but Charlotte had been impatient with things that were meant to be that morning. She needed to take just one of those things—even a small one—and cheat fate with it.

So she'd scooped up the helpless bird and carried it to the house. "What the %#@$ do you think you're doing?" Daniel had hollered after her, inexplicably furious. "They die out of the nest! You'll never save it! It's as good as dead!"

She remembered thinking at the time that he might as well have been talking about their marriage. Perhaps that was why saving that tiny life had become so important.

She didn't dare tell anyone—Daniel, especially—how much time and effort she'd expended keeping the bird alive. Not about feeding it every hour with a toothpick that first week; not about rigging a brace over a bare lightbulb so the box would stay warm enough at night without catching fire—and certainly not about filling a shoe box with sand warm from the morning sun every day so the stupid thing could have a sand bath. Goodness, if anyone knew all that, they'd have her committed. "You're obsessed, Charlotte," they'd say; and they'd probably be right.

What was so darn important, after all, about saving the life of a single tiny bird? But the life had come so cheap—a box of baby cereal and a can of cat food. *A dollar for a life*, she thought, looking at the feathered heartbeat in her hand. *That wasn't so much to pay, was it?*

Chirp. Huey cocked his head and looked up at her, making her smile, and that in itself seemed like a small miracle.

With a rush of feathers that startled her out of her reverie, Huey flew from her hand to the porch railing. He tipped his head this way and that, as if to contemplate the enormity of the world beyond.

"Go on, Huey. Go out there and be a bird."

Chirp.

"Catch your own bugs. Find a girl. Get a life."

Chirp.

Sighing, Charlotte pushed herself out of her chair. The bird was on her shoulder before she was completely erect. "This is ridiculous," she grumbled, walking down the steps toward the big box elder that shaded the porch. "You think I'm going to walk you to this tree for the rest of my life? You're worse than a kid on the first day of kindergarten."

Huey rode her shoulder until they were under the tree, then made a short, awkward flight up to a low-hanging branch, all he was capable of at this age. A light breeze ruffled the down on his chest as he began pecking earnestly at the bark, obeying some mysterious genetic memory.

Charlotte leaned against the trunk and let her mind drift as she watched the beautifully simple business of survival. Hunt, peck, swallow, preen. Not much to it, really. The birds had it down pat. Why did human beings have so much trouble with it?

After a time Huey landed on her head, then hopped down to her hand when she held out her cupped palm. He wriggled into the warmth and made tiny peeping sounds while his bluish lower lids closed up over his bright black eyes. Charlotte felt childishly pleased, because for this one small life, at least, she did everything right. She was perfect.

She walked back up to the porch and placed the bird on the edge of the cardboard carton just as Daniel's truck came roaring back up the drive.

"Huey, get in your box," she said clearly.

When the truck door slammed shut, the bird hopped down into the depths of the box, skittered under a loose paper towel, and went immediately still.

Daniel stomped up the porch steps and dropped into the chair opposite Charlotte's. He ran both hands through a full head of dark hair and looked at her with eyes that looked like winter lake ice in his sun-bronzed face. "The next trip is the last," he said, and Charlotte felt a flutter deep inside, as if Huey were hiding in her stomach. It surprised her a little.

She'd known this moment was coming; they'd both agreed to it; so why was her body faltering when her mind was made up? "You sure you have everything you need?" Such a civilized, practical question, but her voice sounded like someone else's, someone she didn't know.

"I'll be only ten miles away. If I forgot anything, I can always arrange to pick it up later." There was no music in his voice anymore; it fell on the air like a leaden weight and prompted an answering skitter from deep within the box. His eyes shifted down and narrowed. "Don't tell me that stupid bird is still around."

She glanced down at the box, lips pressed together. "He's still around."

"I thought you said he was flying."

"Just a little. He's still learning."

A sharp line appeared at one side of his mouth as he turned his head away. She examined his profile, looking for her husband. "You've been mother hen to that worthless bird for over three weeks. When in the world are you going to let it go?"

"I'm not stopping him. The porch is wide open. He can leave whenever he's ready. It's just too soon."

"You lock him in the mudroom at night."

She shrugged, exasperated that he could argue about the bird at a time like this. "Keller's cats are over here all the time after dark; you know that. They'd make a meal of him in a minute if I left him out here on the porch."

"It's only a sparrow, for Pete's sake," he snapped at her, "and it would have died the day it fell out of its nest if you hadn't interfered."

She folded her hands tightly in her lap and glared at him, wondering if he thought she'd upset the cosmic order of things by saving the life of a single sparrow. "Perhaps you'd like to wring his neck, Daniel," she said in that quiet voice of hers that always made things sound twice as horrifying. "Set things right again."

For an instant he looked genuinely startled, and in that instant Charlotte felt something just barely remembered tug at her insides. But then his face closed tight, like a door slamming, and the feeling passed.

When she looked at Daniel again, his eyes were fixed on the door that went into the house. "There's a hole in that screen. It'll need replacing unless you want the house filled with mosquitoes."

Charlotte looked down at her hands; small, square, capable hands, as adept at mending a screen as they were at cradling the fragile body of an orphaned sparrow. "I can take care of it."

"I know that," he snapped, and she heard the admonition in his tone. That was her crime, she supposed—that she could take care of things, that on the surface, at least, she was as stubborn and resilient as he was.

They looked at each other in a moment of awkward silence, like actors in a bad film who'd both forgotten their lines.

Finally he said, "Any problem with me leaving now?"

Charlotte felt a rocket launch in her stomach, a burst of fire and thrust that burned up all the oxygen in her body. "Well . . . I already put a big roast in the oven," she said so quickly that it sounded breathless. "I guess I didn't think you'd finish so soon . . . I thought you'd still be here for supper . . ."

"I can stay for supper if you like."

She looked down at her lap and shrugged. "Whatever."

His chair squeaked as he got up. "I'll just finish loading up before we eat, then."

After he left the porch Charlotte leaned back in her chair very slowly, realizing for the first time that she'd been perched on the edge of her seat, spine rigid with tension. She exhaled sharply upward, and a wisp of hair stirred on her forehead.

At her feet there was a muffed flutter, and then she felt the tickle of tiny feet dancing tentatively on the back of her hand. She turned her head and looked down at the little brown head cocked comically sideways, the bird's shiny black eye regarding her solemnly. She left him drowsing in the shade on the railing while she went in to finish making supper. He'd be safe there until sunset, at least—the Kellers' cats rarely trespassed before then—and she wanted him outside, getting used to his natural habitat as much as possible. Soon, very soon now, he would have to learn to make his own way in his own world.

The roast had just come out of the oven when Daniel came downstairs carrying a plastic garbage bag so stuffed with clothes the side seams had started to split. He dropped it next to the back door with a thud that Charlotte felt like a gunshot to the heart, then took his customary seat at the oversized kitchen table.

She looked at him with an emptiness in her eyes that went all the way down to her soul, an emptiness she'd never expected to feel. It just didn't seem right, ending seven years of a shared life this way. If marriage had to end at all, it should end noisily, explosively, so you knew when it happened. Theirs had just seemed to fade away gradually, like the bright colors of a quilt hung too many times in the sun. For one frightening instant, she felt the strangest impulse to reach out and grab Daniel and just hang on, as if by holding him physically she could somehow hold them together as well. But that was silly.

"Potatoes?" she asked politely, passing the bowl.

It was almost a relief when the phone rang, interrupting a meal that Charlotte couldn't eat anyway. She answered, listened a few moments to Nancy Keller's distraught voice, murmured a few words of assurance, then hung up with a heavy sigh. "Nancy's oldest boy just sliced his hand open on a can lid. Nothing serious, but it's going to need stitches, and their car won't start. I have to drive them to the hospital."

Daniel watched her from the table as she gathered her purse and keys. "I'll probably be gone by the time you get back," he told her, watching her face with the oddest expression, almost as if he expected her to say something. But what could she say to that?

Her feet seemed rooted to the spot. For some reason, it made her angry that he could leave when she was gone, when he wouldn't have to feel her eyes on his back as he walked away. She turned and left by the back door without saying anything.

The emergency waiting room at the small local hospital was a sterile, sickly white under the glow of fluorescent lighting. Charlotte sat in a vinyl chair facing the window, fidgeting as she watched the light go out of the sky, thinking of all the things she might have said to Daniel, and all the things that Daniel might have said to her.

Thunder rumbled in from the west, and by the time the doctors had put ten stitches and a lollipop in the hand of Nancy's son, big fat drops were hitting the plate-glass window.

"Sorry it took so long," Nancy said, frowning out the window. "Oh no! It's raining already, and I forgot to put the cats in."

Charlotte's eyes fell, closed in sudden, sickening realization, and she dashed for the pay phone on the wall. She didn't know quite how she would ask Daniel to please postpone leaving her long enough to stand guard on the porch over a bird he hated, but as it turned out, she didn't have to. There was no answer when she tried to call home. Daniel didn't live there anymore.

The black windows of an empty house stared at her through the steady slapping of windshield wipers as she pulled into the muddy drive. With her lips pressed so tightly together they carved a white line across her chin, she dashed through the downpour and trotted up the porch steps.

"Huey?" she called, but her voice was lost in the rising wind and the crack of thunder. In the next flash of lightning, she saw a scattering of damp, downy feathers on the porch floor, and for the very first time in her life, Charlotte burst into tears.

"For goodness' sake, Charlotte, get in here before you get soaked." Daniel's voice came though the screen of a window, startling her so badly that she dropped her purse.

"Daniel?"

The house was so dark she couldn't even make out his features on the other side of the screen, and he took a long time before he answered her. "You left the bird on the porch, Charlotte."

She swallowed hard, blinking down at the pathetic jumble of wet, downy feathers.

"I was afraid to leave with him still outside." Daniel was mumbling, almost as if he were apologizing for still being here. "So I've been chasing him all over the porch ever since you left. Dumb thing pecked me nearly to death when I finally caught him, just before the power went out."

She raised her head slowly and stared at the dark shape on the other side of the screen. "You *caught* him?" she whispered.

"I caught him. He's in his box in the mudroom."

Charlotte stood on the open porch, battered by the cold, wind-driven rain, wet hair slapping around her face. He'd caught the bird. He'd stayed here to save the one-dollar bird she couldn't help caring about.

"Charlotte?"

She could hear the confused worry in his voice, probably because she was standing on the porch in the middle of a storm bawling her eyes out like an idiot, but she simply couldn't stop.

"There's no need for that," he mumbled gruffly, awkwardly. "The bird's fine, really. I wouldn't have left him out there for the Kellers' cats, not after all you went through to save him."

"I . . . know . . ." the words came out like hiccups because she was crying so hard.

There was a loud clatter as he bumped a table hurrying in the dark, and then he opened the front door and pulled Charlotte into his arms and let her cry against his chest.

"He was flying around the porch pretty good tonight, Charlotte," he murmured into her hair. "I think we'll be able to set him free soon."

We. He'd said "we." Charlotte smiled through her tears and tasted salt, clinging to Daniel as if she'd never let go, because some things you set free, and some things you just had to try to hang on to.

* * * * *

"Hanging On," by P. J. Platz. Reprinted by permission of Patricia and Traci Lambrecht. All rights reserved. P. J. Platz (Patricia and Tracy Lambrecht) are a successful mother/daughter writing team currently living in Stillwater, Minnesota. They are prolific writers of short stories, novels, and movie scripts, and their work is carried by contemporary women's and family magazines.

How a Skylark Preached a Sermon

Author Unknown

In the 1850s, the news flashed around the world: "Gold has been discovered in Australia—lots of it!" And men from everywhere—especially England—left homes and families—and boarded ships for that vast then unknown continent almost half a world away.

Once there, in the brutal no-holds-barred battles for gold—goodness, kindness, mercy, and God were all but forgotten.

Which is where our 1872 story begins:

* * * * *

Stories, as well as poems, about the skylark abound; but the following story shows the constant love of Englishmen for this truly English bird. There is no such thing as a songbird natural to Australia; there are birds that chatter, and birds that shriek, but no bird that sings. Well, there was a young man who went out from England as a gold digger, and was fortunate enough to make some money, and prudent enough to take care of it. He opened a "store" (a sort of rough shop, where almost anything could be had) at a place called "The Ovens," a noted goldfield about two hundred miles from Melbourne. As he continued to prosper, this young man, like a dutiful son, wrote home for his father and mother, asking them to come out to him, and, if they

possibly could, to bring with them a lark. The old folks agreed, and in due time, with a lark in charge, they boarded ship and left the shores of England.

His father, however, took the change so much to heart that he died; but his mother and the lark landed in sound health at Melbourne and were speedily forwarded to Mr. Wilsted's store at "The Ovens." It was on Tuesday when they arrived, and the next morning the lark's cage was hung outside the hut, and at once the lark began singing. The effect was wonderful. Sturdy diggers—big men with great brown hands—paused in the midst of their work and listened reverently. Drunken diggers left unfinished the blasphemous sentence and looked bewildered and ashamed. Far and near the news spread rapidly: "Have you heard the lark?" "Is it true, mate, that there is a real English skylark up at Jack Wilsted's?"

So it went on for three days, and then came Sunday morning. Such a sight had not been seen since the first spadeful of the golden earth had been turned! From every quarter—east, west, north, and south—from far-off hill and from creeks twenty miles away, came a steady stream of rough, brawny Englishmen, all brushed and washed as decent as possible. The movement was not arranged beforehand, as was plain from the half-ashamed expression on every man's face as he met his acquaintances in the crowd. There they were, however, and their errand was—to hear the lark! Nor were they disappointed. There, perched in his wood-and-iron pulpit, was the little minister, and, as if he knew the importance of the task before him, he plumed his crest, and, lifting up his voice, sang them a sermon, which touched his audience more deeply than perhaps even the bishop himself could have done.

It was a wonderful sight to see those three or four hundred men, some lying on the ground, some sitting with their arms on their knees and their heads on their hands, some leaning against the trees with their eyes closed, so that they might the better fancy themselves at home and in the midst of English cornfields once more; but, whether sitting, standing, or lying, all were equally quiet and attentive; and when, after an hour's steady preaching, the lark ceased, his audience suddenly started off, a little low spirited, perhaps, but on the whole happier than when they came. Yes, and doubtless in many a breast the lark's warble had stirred the memories of the lessons learned in the village school or in the village church at home, and had wakened unuttered longings for those "means of grace" for which they had cared so little when they were within their reach.

So the skylark preached his sermon, and many of his congregation wished that they could have taken him away with them to preach to them in their distant diggings day by day.

"I say, Joe," one digger was heard to say to another, "do you think Wilsted would sell him—the bird, you know? I'd give as much gold dust for him as he weighs and think him cheap."

"Sell him! Not he!" was the indignant answer. "How would you like a fellow to come to our village at home and make a bid for our parson?"

* * * * *

"How a Skylark Preached a Sermon," author unknown. Published in The Youth's Instructor, *August 1872. Text printed by permission of Joe Wheeler (P.O. Box 1246, Conifer, CO 80433) and Review and Herald® Publishing Association, Hagerstown, Maryland.*

Haji, the Walking Fish

Daniel P. Mannix

The maid seemed to have aged years in only a week. As for her employer, when Haji grandly descended the stairs—that was just too much!

* * * * *

It was the swankiest tea of the year, and Father said that I ought to go with the rest of the family. It was a big tea, and automobiles were parked in long lines along the curb so that you might have thought there was a football game in progress. Our car took its place in the long queue to the front door, where two men were opening the car doors and letting out the guests in much the same way keepers at our zoo open the cage doors of the newly arrived animals and shoo them into their new pens.

We were propelled by the mob into the drawing room and up to the receiving line. Here, after shaking hands with the perspiring hostess and her debutante daughter, the crowd flung us aside into a corner behind the piano. A harassed waiter, with the same keeper-feeding-the-livestock manner, shoved a plate with two macaroons and a roll into my hand and an empty cup into my sister's and vanished into the throng. I was about to offer one of the macaroons to my sister when she spied a group of school friends and left me.

Suddenly a moist warm nose was thrust into my hand, and I looked down

into the wistful brown eyes of Prince, the police-dog puppy. He and I were old friends. In the summer we had taken many walks together, but with the opening of college, our comradeship had broken up.

Poor Prince! He was a cheerful friendly person with enormous legs and a tail that was always getting in his way in moments of excitement. His life was a ceaseless series of snubs and "don'ts." He loved to play, but no one ever wanted to play with him. He always lived in hope and trotted eagerly up to anyone he saw, usually to be rebuffed. He looked up gratefully and fondly at me while I scratched his long, floppy ears, and he courteously accepted half the sandwich while I looked about and took stock of the other guests.

Prince and I were on the edge of a group that had gathered about a man whom I recognized as an officer in the British army. He had spent most of his life in India and Indo-China, and Philadelphia hostesses had been making a great lion of him. He was now telling of an expedition he had made into the treacherous salt swamp that fringes Cambodia. He was a natural storyteller, and I was soon as much interested as the rest of the group around him. His experiences had been marvelous—so marvelous, in fact, that he seemed to fear that his audience might doubt him, and so he now and then mentioned references by some authoritative book that verified his statements. We were particularly impressed by the stories of the strange animals and plants that live in the hot, humid wilderness.

"We paddled up the Iriknue Canal, and the wildlife in the trees along the banks was perfectly incredible," he said. "There were thousands of monkeys, great butterflies a foot across, and the most beautiful birds."

I leaned forward, deeply interested.

"Were there any fish in the trees?" I asked.

One of those dead hushes followed. The Englishman stroked the edge of his coffee cup and said nothing for a moment. Then, still without looking at me, he replied, "Everything I have said this afternoon is true. I think that bit of sarcasm was quite unnecessary."

"It wasn't meant as sarcasm," I said with some heat. I could feel that everybody thought I had committed an unpardonable *faux pas*. "There are tree-climbing fish in that part of the world, and I thought that you might have seen some."

"I have never seen nor heard of such things," he said, and rising, walked away, leaving me the center of considerable unfavorable attention.

Prince and I left as soon as possible. This was no place for either of us. We were always getting into some sort of trouble, so we went for a walk and chased rabbits until supper.

That was in autumn, and six months later, when the skunk cabbages had begun to bloom and the skunk family woke up from their winter sleep, and Wag-acha, the raccoon, began to wander along the shores of the creek looking for tadpoles, I had completely forgotten the tea and was busy cleaning out the ponds for the fish. One day while I was wading knee-deep in the muddiest pool, Mother called to me that I was wanted on the telephone.

It was Mark Wilcox, another amateur zoo keeper, who spends most of his spare time hanging about the docks and buying strange beasts that the sailors bring in from their voyages.

"Dan, I'm at customs," he shouted, "and there's a big tin milk can here for you labeled 'Live fish' from Korea. It's from Vice Counsel Chadwick-Collins. Do you know anything about it?"

"No—but," I was thinking, "by George—I might! That Englishman must have found something and sent it to me. Golly, what a break!"

"Say, what are you talking about?"

"Listen, Mark, pay the duty—I'm always paying duty on your crazy stuff! Be quick! And take them to your aunt's and pour the water out of the can into a bathtub. Don't add any fresh water whatever you do. I'll jump in the car and be out as soon as I can."

"All right, but hurry up. It'll take one of us to hold my aunt and the other to watch the fish. The duty is $4.48. Don't forget to bring that in with you too."

The great trouble with living in our place is that it takes a good hour's fast driving to get into town. I arrived at Wilcox's aunt's and was admitted by a maid who seemed to have aged years since our last meeting the week before. From above came the voices of Mark and his aunt, imploring me to hurry up. I raced upstairs and found them sitting on a barricade of furniture heaped up in front of the bathroom door.

"For heaven's sake, what is the matter?" I gasped.

"Your fish," answered Mark. "We've got him locked in the bathroom, and Aunt is scared stiff of him."

"Why, he can't get out of the bathtub, can he?" I asked.

"Oh, can't he! He's been out twice, and the first time he was halfway down the stairs before I got him. The second time he got under Aunt's bed."

Here his aunt joined into the conversation. She was slightly incoherent, but I gathered that of all the strange, unholy, and unpleasant things she had ever seen, that fish led the rest by ample margin. She also added that the sooner it left the house, the better she would feel. The wall of furniture, I was informed, was to keep it from crawling out under the door.

After some trouble, the blockade was lifted, and I entered the bathroom. The fish was lying in the middle of the floor, but when I entered, he slithered off under the washstand. Poked out with a broom, he was seized and returned to the bathtub, where I was able to take a good look at him.

"Haji," as he was afterward named from the Chinese word meaning a supernatural being, was about a foot long, rather eel-like in shape, with a thick, blunt head. He was handsomely marked in grey and silver, and his gracefully moving body gave but little hint of the tremendous strength in his muscular frame.

For a moment he sank to the bottom of the dirty water in which he had come all the way from Korea and lay on the smooth white enamel of the bathtub. Then, with a sudden stroke of his powerful side fins, he shot to the surface, took a deep audible breath of air and sank again.

"Look at that!" I exclaimed. "He has to breathe air just as the book says they do. You know that old joke about the man who trained his pet fish to stay out of water so long that one day it fell in and drowned? Well, that is really true of this fellow. If he couldn't get air, he would drown."

That was too much for Mark's aunt. She left, expressing a wish that the fish, Mark, and I would all be gone when she returned. After a fight that would have given Melville some helpful hints for *Moby Dick,* we got Haji out and into a bucket and started for home.

On the way, Mark told me what had happened before my arrival. He had left the tin containing Haji at the top of the stairs while he pried off the cover. Being unable to see anything except dirty water, he had gone off to get an old fish net that he remembered having seen behind the cellar door. On the way back, he had met his aunt at the foot of the stairs, and as he was gradually leading up to the point of telling her that the bathtub would be in use that evening, she had suddenly grasped his arm with a horrified cry of *Look!*

Down the stairs was coming Haji, all twelve inches of him. He passed them with the air of someone who is going places and doing things, and

Mark retrieved him just as his aunt sank fainting on the lowest step.

Haji was rushed upstairs and hastily dumped into the bathtub, but as Mark forgot to shut the door, Haji was discovered a few minutes later under the bed by a hysterical maid. The idea of a walking fish alarms most people, especially when suddenly met with in the bedroom, and Mark was afraid that Haji was not appreciated. He also thought that I had better cover any aquarium I put our Chinese visitor into.

When at last we reached home, I hurried Haji in his bucket to the fishes' greenhouse and there began to prepare an aquarium for him. He was still in the same water in which he had been shipped, and my first care was to take its temperature and pH level (the acid content). I have a huge wooden tub full of rainwater, as ordinary tap water is bad for fish. I filled a twenty-gallon aquarium from it and then put in a heater attached to a thermostat set for 65 degrees, the temperature of the water Haji was now in. This was much too low, but a sudden change would be fatal, as fish are cold-blooded and their body temperatures are the same as the water about them.

After testing the bucket water, I found that it registered 6.8, and as the pH would not have been changed by the long days en route, I decided that this was the acidity of the water that Haji lived in at home. With acid sodium phosphate, I brought down the high basic pH of my tank. I carpeted the bottom of the tank with fine white sand but used no plants, as this was a hospital aquarium for Haji to recover in.

For several days afterward, I was afraid that my strange Chinese pet would pass on to that other world where so many newly imported animals go. He had the dread ichthyophthiriasis, a sort of fish pneumonia, for he had been chilled during the long sea voyage. Tiny white spots appeared on his fins, which I painted with mercurochrome. At last he recovered and began to swim about his tank instead of lying listlessly on the bottom, took an interest in his food, and became quite lively—in fact, *too* lively.

One day the cook made the mistake of putting his supper—raw hamburger steak—on the glass that covered his tank. Haji saw the juicy, red meat through the glass top, treaded water for a minute just beneath it, and then suddenly leaped upward. There was a crash of breaking glass, and Haji was out again. Unfortunately, the cook had returned kitchenward immediately after leaving the meat and did not see the disaster.

When I returned that evening I found Haji flopping about unhurt amid the broken glass on the greenhouse floor.

I do not like to say anything about my family, but it often seems as if they spend most of their spare time breaking glass in my greenhouse, so when I discovered the broken glass, I went roaring through the house accusing everyone I met. They all swore that they had not been near my old greenhouse and marched out to inspect the damage.

Still complaining, I fitted another sheet of glass over the aquarium, and this time Haji was quicker to act. With the full force of his steel-spring body, he leaped up. *Smash* went the glass, and once more he was on the floor. Speechless, I returned him to the tank amid a chorus of "There now! You're always saying we hurt your old animals, and half the time they do it themselves!"

I was glad when summer came, and Haji was moved out to a pool in the garden. So was Haji. He took on the most beautiful hues in the warm sun and loved to spend hours floating half in and half out of the water. Woe to the luckless caterpillar or beetle that wandered too close to the edge of the pool! Haji would fling himself out on the soft mud bank, seize his prey, and slither back into the water.

His bulldog jaws had tremendous power as Rags, my little dog, found out. Poor Rags had come down for a drink at Haji's pond after a hot day playing with the armadillos in the sandpile. No sooner, however, had he stuck his hot nose into the water than the fish grabbed it, thinking, I suppose, that a new sort of bug had fallen in. Rags yelled the dog equivalent of "Ghosts!" and "Murder!" until I rushed over and separated them.

Rags was not the only one who found Haji startling. We gave a garden party later in the summer, set up tables around the garden, and hoped that somebody would come. After hearing that Nickkies, my skunks, would be locked up, people *did* come, and it was very pleasant to see the women in graceful tea gowns and the men in cool white flannels strolling about the garden. My ponds were covered with water lilies and water hyacinths and were greatly complimented. Several ladies asked what animals were in them— and one found out!

She was sitting on the edge of Haji's pond, and while greeting a friend she had laid a plate containing a stuffed olive on the ground beside her. She was leaning down to recover the olive when the red pepper caught Haji's eye. With a leap he shot out from among the water lilies, snatched the olive, and vanished again. The lady remained motionless for a moment, and then left hurriedly.

We nearly lost Haji once. There had been a heavy thunderstorm, and the garden was flooded. Haji left his pool and wandered about joyfully in the inch or so of water that covered the lawn, picking up worms and drowned insects. The road that runs by the foot of our place became a sea of mud in heavy rains, and three or four cars were stalled there. The owners have assured me—and one fought all through the war—that their emotions, when the tall grass parted and Haji marched down the middle of the road, were indescribable.

Haji has had to quiet down since then. I built a pen around his pool with a sign "Beware of the fish!" which really was not necessary but sounded nice. Anyway, Haji does not seem to mind.

* * * * *

"Haji, the Walking Fish," by Daniel P. Mannix. Published in St. Nicholas, *May 1934. Original text owned by Joe Wheeler. Daniel P. Mannix of Philadelphia was well known during the first half of the twentieth century as the Keeper of the Back-Yard Zoo. His true-life animal stories were carried by popular magazines of his day.*

LARRY GOES TO THE ANT

Effie Ravenscroft

It was the toughest decision of Larry's life, one that would change the course of his life.
Preposterous that a tiny ant could tip the balance. . . .

* * * * *

Larry had come to a decision! The joy of it was in the brightness of his eyes; but the awe of it was in the pallor of his cheeks. With a hand that trembled, he took out his watch. The hands stood at five minutes to ten. In five minutes, his father's morning office hours would be over. Dr. McCleary would then be free from interruption for a period, unless he had an emergency call; and it was this possible interim that Larry intended to make use of for the delivering of what, he acknowledged to himself with a sinking feeling at the pit of his stomach, was going to be a shock.

The thought of the approaching ordeal brought sweat to his brow; and to enable himself to bear those five minutes, he took from his innermost pocket an envelope and held it in his hand. It was the contents of that envelope that had led to the decision that, he felt, was going to shake to its very foundations the McCleary household.

At the end of those awful five minutes, he drew a gasping breath of relief,

put the envelope carefully back into his pocket, and arose. Larry was a stalwart youth, and one of the coolest-headed of the athletes that the local college had graduated at its last term. But as he started down the stairs, his trained and prize-winning legs trembled so that, for the first time since his infancy, he had to grasp the banisters for support.

The other office was without waiting patients, and the inner one was likewise without occupants, so Larry went to the library. A wave of affection so great that it momentarily choked him swept over him as he stood in the door for a moment and looked remorsefully at his father's stately head, crowned by its waves of iron-gray hair, the best-loved head in the town.

Dr. McCleary looked up from the pile of pamphlets on the table.

"Hello, son!" he exclaimed cheerfully. "I was just going to call you. I've decided, after many mental throes," he went on, with a merry twinkle in his eyes, "which college is going to have the honor of conferring another 'Dr. Lawrence S. McCleary' on the world. I've selected the one in Baltimore. It's some distance from home, to be sure," and the doctor's face shadowed, "but you'll take a three-years' course at this one"—he handed Larry a prospectus—"and a postgraduate at Johns Hopkins. You'll thereby do the whole thing in the same city, which I, being old-fashioned, consider an advantage, especially as this particular city contains one of the most famous hospitals in the world. You see, I believe in roots. There's been a Dr. McCleary for six generations, and will be one for six more, I trust. And I intend that the one I contribute shall be the best that money can provide. Does that plan meet with your august approval, son?"

There was an odd undercurrent of wistfulness in the doctor's tone, in spite of its jocularity. And Larry, who'd always shared a bond of sympathetic yet silent understanding with his father, caught the undertone and choked up again.

"Dad," he commenced, almost inarticulately, "there's something—something—" He gathered himself together and finally blurted out in a rush, "Dad, I don't want to be a doctor—I can't be a doctor, Dad! I want to be a newspaper man!"

It might have been a full minute before Dr. McCleary found his voice and replied, but to Larry it seemed an eternity.

"Sit down, son," the doctor said, in the gentle tone of one who is dazed. "Now what is this that you just said? You don't want to be a doctor? There never was an eldest McCleary who didn't want to be a doctor, son. Let's have the whole story. Perhaps it's just a delusion."

Larry shook his head vehemently at the closing remark, for he felt his courage returning under the strengthening influence of the doctor's presence. He leaned forward and looked with the eloquent brown eyes of his mother into the steady gray ones of his father.

"Dad," he said, "this is a crisis, and it's not a time for keeping anything back. I've never wanted to study medicine. Never! And I believe that somehow you knew it before I did; you felt it. I'd never even admitted it to myself until a couple of weeks ago, when all those things from the medical schools began to come in. And, Dad, I've always loved newspapers instinctively; and I didn't realize that until—well, recently. You know I've always tried to read 'em, Dad, ever since I could sit up to one. Every time I hear a newsboy call an 'extra,' or even the regular edition for that matter, an electric shock runs up my spine. Oh, I can't tell you all, Dad! But I'm mad about 'em, just properly mad, that's all; not books, you understand, but papers, the things that represent life right up to the last minute ticked off by the clock!

"And I didn't tell you, Dad, but when you and I went to Washington to that convention, I spent nearly all my time among the papers at the Congressional Library while you were sitting at the feet of the scientists you know. The library has papers from all over the world, Dad, and files that go back to the year one, I guess. You know," he went on, with shining eyes, "it's said to be the greatest newspaper collection in the world. From my way of looking at things, Dad, the newspaper man is the man who touches life in its broadest sense."

Dr. McCleary's ruddy face had become the color of cold ashes. He looked at his son curiously and then smiled somewhat wanly.

"So does a doctor, son; so does a doctor," he said slowly.

He brushed a hand across his forehead.

"This is an awful blow, Lawrence—we will be frank, as you said. The eldest McCleary has always been a doctor, you know. There's never been any question about it for generations; somehow we've come to think that the world expects it of us, and that the rule is as fixed as the other vital laws of the universe. For several years I've been planning finances so that you could have the best and broadest advantages. And lately, well, I get tired sometimes. The practice is heavy and the responsibility great; and I realize at this moment how I have been looking forward to the support of my boy, the next Dr. McCleary.

"But you're right, son. I've felt rather than known all along that your heart wasn't in it. But a newspaper man, son, why a newspaper man? I wonder how it happened! No McCleary was ever remotely connected with a paper. I must say," he continued, as if to himself, "that the average reporter doesn't impress me. In yesterday's paper, for instance, one of them announced that *pellagra* is the medical name for hookworm! Being the editor of the school paper hasn't gone to your head, has it, Larry?" he concluded, with a hopeful note in his tone.

"Not a bit of it, Dad!" Larry replied emphatically. "Maybe this has, though."

He took from his pocket the envelope and laid it, superscription side up, upon the table. In conservative and impressive lettering in the upper left-hand corner was the inscription *The Morning Tribune*. Dr. McCleary extracted the contents, and the latter proved, to his amazement, to be a narrow slip of blue paper which said: "Pay to the order of Lawrence McCleary fifteen dollars."

"That's for an idea I sent to *The Tribune*, Dad," Larry explained, "just the bare idea, you understand. And it was my first attempt to break in; and at the time I meant that it should be my last attempt, too, but—I felt like a traitor to you, Dad. But I had the idea, and I just couldn't keep it in; so I thought I'd have one try, just one. Honest, I thought *The Tribune* would squelch me, and I'd be glad to quit."

Dr. McCleary stared down at that fatal blue slip for fully three minutes. Then he cleared his throat.

"Lawrence," he said, "suppose you go out and prowl around the garden till I call you. I'll be ready to talk business to you then."

Larry went out, and with his cap pulled down over his face, sat down in front of the old sundial that for generations had served the McClearys as a focus for their attention when they had weighty problems to solve. Fully a half hour elapsed before his father called him; and by that time, Larry himself had made up his mind to something. When he arose and started slowly toward the house, there was a perceptible droop in his stalwart shoulders.

He did not wait for his father to speak.

"Father," he said (and Dr. McCleary started, for it was the first time in his experience that one of his motherless sons had addressed him as "Father"), "it's all over. Why, I wouldn't grieve you that way for anything in the world! Nothing that I might do in life would compensate me for it. I'll be a doctor, Father, and I'll be a good one too!"

"Not so fast, son; not so fast!" the doctor exclaimed cheerfully. "You'll be what you were cut out to be; I haven't any right to deny you that privilege, even if I am your dad. But we'll make a sporting proposition of it, son. In other words, I shall require you to *prove* to me that you were cut out to break all the McCleary traditions and be a newspaper man instead of a doctor. I'll put it to you this way: if you can get on *The Tribune*, I'll not only accept the situation, but I'll give you my blessing, and it'll be from the bottom of my heart; but understand, I stipulate that it must be *The Tribune*."

Larry's shoulders straightened magically; a smile crossed his face, and he started to speak. But his father raised his hand.

"Wait a minute! This is a crisis with both of us, and we're going to play fair. I know what you are up against, and you don't. *The Tribune* is and always has been my ideal paper; it is, in fact, one of the very few papers for which I have respect. I would consider any connection with it an honor. But

I happen to know something of its innermost workings. Because, my son, you are not the only young gentleman in this town who aspires—or has aspired—to the excitement of newspaper life. The sons of three of my patients and friends have done likewise in the last five years. All of them aspired to *The Tribune,* and none of them met with success. They were able to get on other papers, but they haven't made *The Tribune* yet, and probably never will.

"That paper uses the utmost discrimination in the selection of its men. Nothing ordinary will do, for when a man is put on *The Tribune,* he is there for life, if he cares to stay; and he is pensioned after a certain number of years' service. It has made some of our most prominent writers. It has an application file that reaches nearly to the ceiling, I suspect, and it fills its rare vacancies from that. You may think that you have an open sesame in that check, but you haven't. I will admit, though, that you may have in it a wedge that will open the way for a personal interview. I want to warn you, though, that Colonel Larrabee has the reputation of being a sort of man-eating tiger unless— well, unless."

The eager light of battle had come into Larry's eye. He unconsciously took a grip on his belt and went through a series of motions like a knight girding himself for a fray in which he meant to conquer. His father observed it all and smiled quietly and in a way that suggested a lurking opinion that the seventh Dr. Lawrence McCleary was not yet lost to the family.

"When shall I start, Dad? You are master of ceremonies now," Larry asked.

"*The Tribune* is a morning paper," the doctor replied thoughtfully. "If you leave tomorrow on the seven o'clock train, you will be in the city in an hour and a quarter. That will give you time to freshen up before your interview, supposing that you get an interview," he concluded, with a smile that was half mischievous, half sad.

* * * * *

"Colonel Larrabee will see you now, Mr. McCleary. Will you step this way?" said a composed voice at Larry's elbow. Had Larry been familiar with that voice, he would have detected in it a note of respect and admiration. For the very capable young woman who guarded from intrusion Colonel Willard Larrabee, owner and publisher of the powerful *Tribune,* felt both admiration and respect for anyone who was going to be granted an interview with that grand vizier at ten o'clock in the morning.

When Larry arose, his heart began to pound with such excitement that he was sure its beats were quite audible to the young woman and everyone else in the vicinity. For he was hearing again his father's parting words: "Remember, son, it's a gentlemen's bargain: *The Tribune* or the medical school." And he would have been vastly relieved could he have seen himself as he was seen at that moment, a perfectly composed young man, unmistakably both a gentleman and an athlete, a combination which is bound to be attractive to anyone.

A large person swung around in a revolving chair and glanced at Larry for possibly the fraction of a minute; whereupon Larry felt as though he had been subjected to an application of the X-ray. But the large person spoke; and the quality of the voice that proceeded from the grim mouth was such that Larry felt as if the X-ray had been followed by a soothing narcotic.

"Good morning, Mr. McCleary," Colonel Willard Larrabee said. "And what can I do for you, sir?"

"You can put me on *The Tribune*, sir," Larry promptly replied. And the sound of his own voice amazed him: entirely respectful, it was yet entirely natural, and, moreover, entirely confident. No one could have suspected from its sound that Larry felt himself to be facing his life's crisis; that he was, figuratively speaking, standing before the door whose closing upon him meant condemnation to a life's work with which he had no sympathy, to express it mildly.

Again Colonel Larrabee looked at him. Another expression had replaced the gimlet quality of his eyes, an expression that was half quizzical, half something else, and in its entirety gave the impression that the colonel was going to indulge in something amusing at somebody's expense. That look had a peculiar effect upon Larry. He experienced the same sensations that he always had on the days when it became necessary for him to prove once more to his friends and fellow citizens that he was their star runner. His heart magically quieted, and he sat tight.

"Is that all?" the colonel asked quietly. "Would you believe it, Mr. McCleary, we quite frequently have requests like that here on *The Tribune*? Usually, though, we get them in writing; the applicants don't get past the City Editor to me. Your card, however, rather interested me; it had a weight of its own, you know. By the way, here it is." He handed Larry the "card," the envelope containing *The Tribune's* check. "*The Tribune*," he went on, "is not in the habit of purchasing ideas recklessly; but it can always use an exceptionally good man; an *exceptionally* good one, understand."

He suddenly took out his watch and looked at it.

"Now, Mr. McCleary," he continued briskly, "what paper are you from? How much and what kind of experience have you had? Of course you are sure that you can write, so I won't ask you about that. Can you get the news? You've got the physique; have you got the rest?"

Larry swallowed hard.

"I have had no experience, Colonel Larrabee," he said. And again his voice sounded perfectly natural. "My sole recommendation is that you thought one of my ideas worth buying, and that I believe I was cut out for the work."

The colonel's eyebrows suddenly threatened to disappear into his hair.

"Ah?" he exclaimed, and for a moment said nothing more. And for many a year thereafter, "Ah" spoken as an interrogation was to Lawrence S. Mc-Cleary the most expressive, most cutting word in the English language.

"Who told you, Mr. McCleary, that *The Tribune* is a kindergarten? Nobody, of course. You didn't need to be told—you knew it! Now, the City Editor hasn't any patience with cubs; won't have 'em around him, in fact. But personally, I don't object to an occasional cub if he's got a good physique. In newspaper work, it's not all how well you can write, not by any means! It's how long and how hard you can hustle for news, how long you can go without your dinner before your stomach caves in, etc. As I said before, your physique and your 'card' recommend you for a try-out, anyway. So we'll see what you can do. You go out and hunt me up a nice story about the city's first public school: where it was, and who ran it; who attended it, and what became of all of 'em, the master included. Arrange for some pictures too. You make me a nice story out of that, and we'll see what we'll see."

Larry arose. It seemed to him that a thousand joy bells were ringing in his ears. Poor Dad! The door hadn't shut, after all! For the first time his composure almost deserted him.

"Colonel Larrabee, I appreciate—" he began.

"So you do," the colonel interrupted blandly, and shot his chair halfway around.

Larry, accepting this unmistakable dismissal, started for the door. With his hand on the knob, he stopped and turned.

"How soon must the copy be in, sir?" he asked.

The colonel looked over his shoulder; and now there was no mistaking his expression: it was one of almost impish amusement.

"Oh, in two or three days," he replied. And the revolving chair shot all the way around.

Larry was smiling to himself when, a few minutes later, he entered the nearest drugstore and opened the directory.

Two or three days for a story like that! he thought. *I must have looked like a dub! Why, it's easy, easy! Poor Dad!*

Presently, he emerged from the drugstore and boarded a streetcar. Twelve minutes later, he swung briskly from the platform at a certain corner and ascended the steps of a glistening white building which, long and low, was set in the midst of much trim greenery. Within, a short young man and then a tall young woman were encountered in turn; and by them *The Tribune's* latest acquisition was passed on into a pleasant, peaceful apartment where a pleasant and peaceful-looking man occupied a substantial chair at one end of a table upon which was a clutter of papers. He smiled approvingly if inquiringly as the very good-looking young man advanced upon him; whereupon the said young man responsively glowed.

"Is this Mr. Van Deusen?" Larry inquired.

"It is," replied the superintendent of public schools; and he extended his hand, but did not rise.

"I am from *The Tribune*, Mr. Van Deusen," Larry commenced (and a thrill ran through him as he heard his own words). "And I wanted to see if you would oblige me with some information about the city's first public—"

"There's the door, young man—use it!" And Van Deusen, on his feet now and his face white with anger, pointed to the petrified Larry the way out. There was menace in the gesture; it indicted a restrained desire to force the issue of the door upon the startled young man.

This sudden metamorphosis of an urbane gentleman into a would-be (and obviously capable!) pugilist, rendered Larry, after the first start of surprise, incapable of movement, of inquiry, of protest. Van Deusen surveyed his helpless amazement with an eye glassy from emotion, and then suddenly choked out: "First assignment?"

Larry merely nodded.

"Well," Van Deusen went on, "you are the twenty-third person *The Tribune* has sent here on that fool's errand. The joke may be on you, but the outrage is on me!"

Larry felt himself turn pale; he did not know, however, that his mouth fell open and so remained; this mortifying fact was thrust upon his consciousness later.

Van Deusen continued to survey him in silent rage; but presently a softening glimmer came into his eyes, doubtless compelled there by the edifying spectacle of utter dejection presented by Lawrence S. McCleary Jr.

"Sit down, young man, sit down!" he exclaimed.

Larry sat down. Mr. Van Deusen, however, did not sit down. He continued to stand, and Larry was bitterly sure that he did this that he might glower the more forcefully upon the object of his displeasure. Larry was relieved to observe, though, that he put his muscular-looking hands beneath his coattails and played a flapping accompaniment to the caustic speech that he proceeded to deliver.

"Young man," said the superintendent, "if you possess such a thing as a memory, kindly exert it for the purpose of recalling that some forty years ago this fair city was devastated by fire. Now I, of course, wouldn't expect you or your illustrious predecessors on this assignment to have your valuable mind space cluttered up with a mere incident of this kind. But it so happens that this was the most destructive fire in the history of these United States of America. It raged for two days and two nights; engaged the attention of the whole civilized world; destroyed almost one third of the city; left more than seventy thousand persons homeless. In consideration of these rather unusual details, you may have condescended to make a note of it along with the famous baseball scores. Also it destroyed nearly eighteen thousand buildings and—here we reach our issue—with them all school records whatsoever. Therefore, young man, nobody knows anything about the first public school. Nobody ever *can* know anything about the first public school. I myself would give a pretty penny to know something about it.

"You're the butt of a joke, young man. That's *The Tribune*'s stock 'decoy' for all the cubs who think they are 'called' to journalism and *The Tribune*. And this is the last time I am going to explain that fact, positively the last! I don't know what *The Tribune*'s idea is, I'm sure. Perhaps it wants to see how far each one will go on a blind trail. Well, the farthest any one of the twenty-two went was this office. They all began here and ended here, just as you'll do. But the joke's ceased to be a joke at this end; and if you don't tell your editor so, I shall. In fact, I did tell him at the eighteenth man; but this time I'll make a warning of it."

He ceased speaking, probably because of the evident circumstance that his audience had wilted to the last possible degree. But he continued to flap his coat-tails and glare at the offending one. And it was here that Larry, essaying speech, discovered to his further humiliation that his mouth was open.

"Twenty-three?" he managed to blurt out.

"Twenty-three!" the superintendent acidly agreed. Then suddenly one hand moved itself to his vest pocket and came out filled.

"Have a cigar, boy," he said kindly, "and walk a few squares to the park and sit there and commune with nature until you recover. You seem to be harder hit than the others; anyway, they laughed it off. Perhaps you're not a bluffer; you're showing that you care. Some men wouldn't like that, but it happens that I do. If you really need a position, come to see me in a week; I'm busy now. And remember this, my boy, journalism has no reward except itself."

Larry did not smoke, had never smoked, intended never to smoke; but Larry did not know this at that moment. The world was a blank, the rosy, smiling, promising world of a few minutes ago. So he mechanically took the cigar, choked out a "Thank you, sir," and made his exit. In the same dazed way he made for the nearest park, selected the first bench that impressed itself upon him because of its isolation, and dropped upon it.

The colonel's "joke" had doubtless not appeared as a joke exactly to any of Larry's "illustrious predecessors"; but to Larry it was an actual tragedy. *The Tribune* or the medical school! And now it must be the latter. Anyway, his failure would bring joy at home; and his dad wouldn't guy him about it, because his dad wasn't that sort. How he wished that he could see him.

He put his elbow upon his knee, dropped his disconsolate head into his hand, and fell to surveying the gravel walk. And presently, he became aware that he was not the only agitated creature in that vicinity; for the small space encompassed by his vision was the scene of great excitement to a creature of another world. Within it, a small black ant ran wildly about, stopping now and then at one spot, only to rush off to another, from which she would depart in undiminished haste after having inspected it from every possible angle.

"If I didn't know," Larry observed, "that the ant's high order of intelligence prohibits insanity (according to Messrs. Spencer and Hearn), I'd say that little beast down there had slipped a mental cog."

Just then the "little beast" arrived at a small mass of something resembling dried lime, subjected it to the usual detailed inspection, and then began to remove it atom by atom. Apparently, she believed that the treasure she sought was within the mass, and was to be gotten at only by the painstaking removal of the outward debris. So insignificant was the deposit that no human eye would have observed it under ordinary circumstances; but to the small black worker, it was obviously a mountain of difficulty. All alone there she toiled on the path, and how long Larry watched her, fascinated, he did not know. Once, though, he laughed, shamefacedly enough, to find himself sweating in sympathy with her gigantic endeavors.

Obviously, too, she expected the approach of something, whether hostile or friendly Larry could not determine by her actions; for at frequent intervals she left the immediate scene of her endeavors, reconnoitered carefully in all directions, and then returned to her task. At last, one of these quests was successful. Another ant approached and was met by the first one; an excited consultation ensued, and the pair started off toward the lime, the first one hurriedly and the second one slowly and reluctantly. The latter inspected the "find," another consultation followed, and the second insect departed in a manner ludicrously resembling "flouncing." The first little worker followed for some distance, hesitated, and then returned to her lonely and, as Larry believed, scorned and flouted task.

Finally, after human minutes that were perhaps ant years, she reached what she sought—a tiny bit of the deposit presenting, to Larry's eyes, no point of difference from the discarded debris. The excavator evidenced great excitement at her success, executing about the "find" what looked to Larry strangely like a war dance. She then took firm hold of the treasure, which was three times larger than herself, and began a toilsome journey toward some unseen and distant Mecca. Her method of progress consisted of a sixteenth-inch pull, a halt to regain energy, another pull, and so on.

During one of her reconnoitering trips, which for some reason she continued, Larry (who was now observing for a definite reason) moved her burden backward upon the path of its toilsome passage. The insect's distress was pathetic. Frantically she ran about, seeking the lost; and, finding it, she recommenced its transportation with a determination unshaken by the incalculable (to her) distance that had been lost.

Larry whistled in admiration.

"What a game little brute! Absolutely can't discourage her!" he exclaimed.

Having thus delivered himself aloud, he became aware that his face was hot; an instant later, he realized that he had blushed.

"Lawrence S. McCleary, would-be newspaper man," he said bitterly (yes, he was talking to himself), "you take off your hat to that ant and then get up and follow her example! She's a better man than you are any day in the week! The scrap she wanted was under a mountain of debris; nobody knew whether it was actually there or not. But did she let any one come along and rage at her and say, 'Impossible! It's not there! You can't do it! It can't be done!'? She went on the supposition not that it couldn't be done, but that it could. And she hustled and kept on hustling even when you threw her back; and she'll keep right on hustling too!

"And so will you, Lawrence S. McCleary! You get off this bench and hustle on that assignment! No wonder you've an 'S' in your name! It ought to stand for sluggard—anybody that can be influenced to crawl off and sit down as easily as you can before you've even had a try at it! You can't be a road maker or a bridge builder, or a timber cutter, or an agriculturist, or anything else that Spencer says the ant is; but maybe you'll turn out to be a passable reporter, if you keep your mind on that ant!"

"When you're talkin' to yourself, you're keepin' bad company, sonny," drawled a voice in close proximity.

Larry looked around and then raised his cap in respectful salute to the many years that had seated themselves beside him.

"I believe I was talking to myself," he admitted ruefully, "but I don't do it often. I was discoursing on ants."

"Ants?" the newcomer repeated, quite without surprise. "Well, ants is wonderful creeters. Seems to me they've always got themselves in trainin'. Whyfore do they always be buildin' their houses right in people's paths where they're sure to be knocked down every other minnit? Why, just to make themselves strong 'gainst setbacks! I'm a great hand for readin', and I've read how an ant always comes out on top, no matter what she's run up against. They do say she can run a tunnel through solid rock. But what gets me is she knows all about raisin' mushrooms, which is mor'n I do. I tried raisin' 'em in my cellar, but I come out at the little end o' the horn; which shows I ain't as much sense as a despised little ant."

Larry had turned and was surveying his companion with frank interest; for in the last few minutes, Larry had become a person with one idea—if he could but get on a faint scent on that public-school business, just a scent! Nothing ever just "happens"; mightn't this chance acquaintance who was "a great hand for readin' " be a kindly trick of fate?

"I wonder, sir," he inquired eagerly, "if you couldn't tell me something about the city's first public school?"

But the old man unhesitatingly shook his head.

"I ain't been in these parts but about sixteen years," he said. "Come up here to live with my daughter. An' I don't remember readin' nothin' about that." Then he asked somewhat wistfully, "Got any tobacker, sonny? I'm clean out."

Larry smiled in spite of his disappointment. He withdrew the superintendent's cigar from his pocket and proffered it.

"Will this do?" he asked.

The old man's eyes glistened as he smelled the offering.

"I don't often git a cigar, 'specially a good one like this," he said. "I'm mighty sorry I can't tell you what you want to know." He looked up at Larry regretfully, observed him shrewdly for a moment, and then added, with a droll expression: "You seem all worked up about it, sonny. Now it does appear to me that if a common, underfoot ant can tunnel through rock, a likely lad like you ought to be able to find out about that school. I'm a mighty old man, sonny, an' I ain't made what you'd call a howlin' success out o' life. An' I can look back now an' see how, in tight places, I might have got a hunch from some mighty low-to-the-ground things if I'd been a mind to."

At this bracer Larry arose, and there was determination in the act.

"That's it exactly—just what I was telling myself when you came along," he agreed.

He raised his cap in farewell and started off in a hurry.

"Sonny, come back! I just thought o' somethin'!" the old man shouted. And Larry promptly retraced his steps.

"I beat up my mind, 'count o' you givin' me this cigar," the old man commenced excitedly, "an' I remember readin' something in somethin' or other that somethin' called The Old Settlers' 'Sociation had been broke' up; an' somebody was give' a medal testifyin' that he was the oldest livin' man born in this city. I took notice because he was older 'n me. Now, if you could find one o' them old settlers, sonny!"

Larry gripped the gnarled old hand hard and shook it. "Thank you! I'm off!" he exclaimed.

Twenty minutes later, Larry was seated at a table in the public library, rapidly scanning and turning the pages of the most recent edition of *The Daily News Almanac.*

"Not there!" he murmured, when the last page had been thus scanned. He sat back for a moment, his face tense and pale. *I'll have to get the back numbers,* he thought; *and that'll take time, time, endless, precious time! I never realized before what an important thing time is, not even on field days!*

After he had assured himself many times over that the attendant was in reality a snail though she looked like a human, he found himself in possession of twelve red-bound volumes. Minute after minute he bent over this unaccustomed task, feverish with excitement one moment, cold with discouragement the next. A dozen times he caught himself thinking, *All this trouble for nothing! Didn't Van Deusen and twenty-two others tell you that you couldn't do it? Get on the next train and go home and forget it.* But he answered himself with the admonition: *Keep your mind on the ant, sluggard—keep your mind on the ant, and move the debris! What you want is here somewhere, even if you can't see it!*

In the middle of the volume of the twelfth year back, he suddenly stooped closer. There before him, inconspicuously yet unmistakably there, was a notice of a meeting of The Old Settlers' Association, and it included the name of the secretary! Larry copied it with a shaking hand, and with all possible speed made for the outside and a directory. By all the laws of nature and habit, he should have been hungry; but the thought of food never entered his mind.

"Pierre Dubreuil! What great luck that it wasn't William Jones and a needle in a haystack!" He congratulated himself.

But the directory blandly declined to produce a Pierre Dubreuil. It surrendered only one Dubreuil, Alonzo; and according to its testimony, this gentleman conducted a detective agency in a neighborhood necessitating a fifteen-minutes' ride! Only that one chance, and that the slimmest kind of a one! Larry stifled a groan as he faced this fact. Then he boosted himself with the reminder, "It might be a whole lot worse, sluggard! This Dubreuil's a detective and will know everybody in the city."

Alonzo Dubreuil, Esq., weighed all of two hundred pounds, and evidently hadn't a minute to spare in the businesslike-looking office at which Larry arrived in due time.

Mr. Pierre Dubreuil? No, he was not a relative. In fact, Alonzo had never heard of Pierre. Wait a minute, though. If memory served him correctly, there had been a Dubreuil on the police force, whether Larry's quarry or not he could not say. And unless he was mistaken, this Dubreuil had been retired about, well, say seven years before. A moment's further cudgeling of memory produced the belief that Policeman Dubreuil had lived on Eastern Avenue; but about this fact Alonzo was by no means certain.

You're just moving the debris, Larry, remarked the weary-looking youth who boarded a car marked Eastern Avenue; at which muttering the conductor not unnaturally observed him with speculation in his eye. For many weary minutes, Eastern Avenue's stores and drugstores yielded up no information of a Dubreuil of any name or calling whatsoever. And Larry halted at last in front of a small notion store and looked with unjust animosity at its creditable display of gingham aprons and sweeping caps.

I'm on a fool's errand, just as Van Deusen said. But I'll quit here. This is my last try! so he informed himself as the clanging gong announced his entrance.

Mr. Dubreuil? Yes, indeed! She (the proprietress) and he had "lived neighbors" for years, otherwise she would not have known of his existence; he was a very quiet man, and never talked about himself or his business. But he had moved away three years before, and she did not know his address. Was his name "Pierre"? Alas, she did not know; she had never heard.

What do I want now, I wonder? Larry, outside, interrogated himself. *For a good guess, I'll say an expressman.*

Back into the little shop he went, and elicited the cheering information that the nearest expressman was "down street one block and to the right one block." Where the expressman was concerned, fortune smiled upon Larry at last. He had indeed moved Policeman Dubreuil's folks. No, he didn't know his first name, but he could get his address from his old books. When forthcoming, the new address proved to be within walking distance; but Larry's knees and empty stomach and excitement forbade walking.

"I almost wish I'd never seen an ant," he informed the atmosphere, as he impatiently waited for his car. "It's a plain case of ignorance being bliss. If there'd been anything in what I'm doing, wouldn't some other fellow have done it long ago?"

The woman who opened the door to him at the given address shook her head. Mr. Dubreuil had not lived there for a year. No, she did not know either his first name or his present address; she could not even say that he was still living, as he was very old and had been ill. The door closed unceremoniously upon a very dejected youth.

Now, I wonder what that ant would do in the face of this setback? Larry inquired of himself. *Dubreuil may not be living; if he is living, he may not be Pierre; if he is Pierre, he may not know a blessed thing about the first public school. Well, the ant would just hang on like grim death,* he answered himself. *I'm wound up now, and couldn't stop if I wanted to. Now the woman said Dubreuil had been ill; therefore me for the nearest drugstore!*

Larry had guessed—or, rather, reasoned—correctly. The clerk remembered having filled the Dubreuil prescriptions, which had been numerous. The files yielded the name of the attending physician, and the phone yielded the information that the said doctor was out; he would be back in ten minutes, however, as he had an office appointment, and the patient was waiting even then. Then for an eternity of suspense, Larry sat still and champed the bit. When he again took down the receiver, his hand was icy cold.

Yes, the doctor would certainly give him Mr. Dubreuil's present address. But who required it? Ah, a representative of *The Tribune*? Just a moment. The address came across the wire clearly; and then Larry, his heart in his throat, inquired, "Is Mr. Dubreuil's name 'Pierre'?"

"Pierre, certainly," was the crisp retort; and Larry actually fell away from the phone.

Twenty minutes later, a rosy-cheeked matron was proudly informing a trembling representative of the press (for Larry so considered himself) that her father had indeed been secretary of The Old Settlers' Association. When it had disbanded, he had been given a medal testifying that he was the oldest living man who had been born in the city.

Then Larry braced himself; for the answer to his next question meant either glorious success or crushing defeat—meant, he believed, journalism or the medical school. Did—did she suppose her father could know anything about the city's first public school? The matron laughed.

"I think," she said, "that he could tell you even the exact number of nails it took to build that school. It is the subject nearest his heart, his dearest memory of the old days." He could be found at the Walnut Street Police Station, doubtless.

Larry could never give a clear account of the next few minutes. He always maintained that he neither rode nor walked to that police station; he floated. He must have entered in a conventional manner, however, for his advent excited no commotion whatsoever. He still could not grasp the fact of a success in the face of the seemingly impossible, success for him where twenty-two others had failed!

In such a mental and physical condition was he that he was again surprised at the normal sound of his voice when he inquired for Mr. Dubreuil. He was directed to the sergeant's desk; and when he beheld the manner of man who was occupying the chair, the cap he had removed was crammed into his pocket, instinctive homage to a well-spent life. That Pierre Dubreuil's years were many, he of course knew; that these years were all on the credit side of his life's account was proved by the compact strength of the proudly erect frame, the ruddy glow beneath the dark skin, the clearness of the keen but kindly dark eyes.

Would Mr. Dubreuil perhaps talk to a representative of *The Tribune* about the city's first public school? *Would* he! His sparkling eyes attested to the pleasure it would be to so talk. Just wait until he had had a chair brought in. And when the chair had been brought, he did not talk, he discoursed, glowing with pleasure at his own performance. He told exactly where the school had been; he gave unhesitatingly the names of the teacher and all his fellow pupils—alas, that he should be the sole survivor of that little band! With all sorts of quaint touches—for he was of French-Indian descent—he described the primitive furniture that had been made from packing-cases, etc. He agreed, with obvious pride, to the publication of his photograph, and one of The Old Settlers' medal, and of his children and grandchildren. And if the young man would come out to his house that evening, he could give him more details and some old daguerreotypes.

Surely no cub reporter ever had so satisfactory a subject. And when Larry was at last ready for departure, he was outfitted with notes that were complete in themselves, and with a sketch of the schoolhouse which he had made under

Dubreuil's direction. With the old settler's eloquence thus verbatim, Larry had no misgivings as to the creditable writing of the story.

Outside the station, he consulted his watch. Four forty-five! One last favor this disciple of an ant now prayed. It was that Colonel Larrabee would be at *The Tribune* office when he arrived. And it was granted him. Colonel Larrabee was still there and he would see Mr. McCleary.

The colonel had turned his chair until he faced the door when Larry entered, and his expression indicated that his thoughts were highly amusing. But somehow the twinkle in his eyes became less evident after a second's inspection of *The Tribune*'s latest aspirant. For the expected air of dejection and injury was not apparent about this cub. He looked exhausted, but he bore himself very erectly, and there was a refreshing briskness about him; and in his frank eyes there was—yes—a twinkle that out-twinkled the colonel's own twinkle. But his tone was quietly respectful, with not the faintest tinge of anything else.

"I just wanted to ask you, sir," he said, "how much you require about the city's first public school? I have all the details and a sketch of the school, and have arranged for a number of pictures."

"What's that, McCleary? You say you have that story? *Impossible!*" The colonel's tone was sharp.

The triumphant cub handed him the sketch and his notes. The colonel looked at them, looked at them again, and then looked at Larry.

"Tell me—all," he said simply.

And Larry told him—all except the ant's part in his success. At the end, the colonel leaned back and laughed until he was almost beyond the power of articulation.

"McCleary," he said, "you've blown up *The Tribune*'s stock decoy and made me a lot of trouble. I invented it myself years ago, and it has never failed. I'll never find another like it."

He held out his hand and smiled; and it was a very human, very winning smile.

"You're hired, my boy," he said, "and at eighteen per. That's an unheard-of salary for a cub on *The Tribune;* the few that we've had have never started on over ten, and most were glad to start on nothing. But I'm going to take you under my personal charge; I have plans for you. By the way, McCleary, how badly do you need this job? Be frank. What made you hang on after that wet blanket Van Deusen handed you? He phoned me how near he came to punching your head, and made dire threats into the bargain. But you look hungry, my boy; is it economy or enthusiasm?"

Larry looked startled, and then suddenly blurted out, "Why, I haven't had anything to eat since supper last night! Was too excited to eat breakfast. Drank a cup of coffee, thinking I'd have some breakfast after I saw you, sir. I believe—in fact, I must be hungry. As to how badly I need the job—well, just let me explain, sir."

When the tale had been told, the colonel walked over and laid his hand on his new reporter's shoulder.

"We'll make it twenty per," he said quietly. "You're the kind we want. You've proved it. And—" he exploded with mirth again—"we'll send a copy of your 'special' to Van Deusen by a special messenger, as a peace-offering and promise of future immunity from annoyance. I'm going to let you sign it too."

Larry sent a telegram that night—"On *Tribune;* home Monday."

But there was nothing of his achievement in the air when, having arrived by the earliest train, he walked up the path with a bundle of papers under his arm. There were two reasons for this. One was the sobering thought of what his success would mean to his father; the other had developed on his homeward journey. He had been reviewing his experiences a bit complacently, it must be confessed, when he suddenly brought his fist down upon his knee. "You chump!" he exclaimed under his breath. "Will you tell me where your wits were, that, when you found Dubreuil was a policeman, you didn't go straight to the police department to find him instead of chasing yourself all over town?" It was a wholesomely humiliating and steadying reflection.

As soon as Larry's foot struck the porch, Dr. McCleary himself threw open the screen door. They clasped hands without a word, and then, arm in arm, went to the library. Larry spread open *The Tribune* and pointed out to the doctor his double page, illustrated, signed "special." And the doctor read every word of it and looked at the pictures from every point of view. When he turned to Larry, his eyes were bright.

"I'm proud of you, son," he said.

"But thereby hangs a tale, Dad," Larry replied eagerly. And he told him as he had told the colonel. But he told his father what he had not told his editor, that is, how he might have done it better, and about the ant; about how the little insect's indomitable faith and energy and pluck had been his shame and his inspiration.

"But, Father," he ended (and again the doctor looked startled at the unfamiliar title), "now that I've got what I wanted, I find that I can't keep it. I love it with all my heart. But since I've been away under such circumstances, I find that I must love you with a whole lot more than my heart. So I'm going to explain to the colonel and resign at the end of my first week. Maybe when I've taken my degree, he'll let me write an occasional article, and that'll do."

It was because of Dr. McCleary's emotion that he choked twice before he spoke; and that, when speech did come, it came in the terse slang of the times.

"Forget it!" he blurted out. "Why, you've proved your case beyond all doubt; proved it beyond any point I expected of you! And, son, that little ant has averted a double tragedy in the McCleary household. I'm an old man, son, and have seen much of life, and to me a human being in the wrong place is a tragedy. I was so upset by the turn things had taken that I telegraphed your brother Ted (couldn't wait to write): 'Would you like to be a doctor?' The scamp telegraphed back: 'Hurrah! Homeward bound!'

"He came home on the next train, galloped up the street, and actually wept on my shoulder. If we are to believe him—and I certainly do—he was born with the desire to study medicine. Kept it to himself, because the honor was destined for you. When the telegram came, he almost collapsed before my eyes. Certainly, I am a rich man in my two fine sons, a doctor, and, I believe, an eventual editor, both the sort that the country needs."

"Why, Dad!" Larry exclaimed. "I'd have seen it if I hadn't been blind! I've thrown Ted out from among your books time without number. Couldn't think what a coming lawyer wanted to be reading medicine for. Why, Dad—" he faltered and grew white under his tan. He realized suddenly that all of them had been under a mighty tension. His father saw.

"Ted's across the hall," he said.

Ted was, indeed, across the hall, sitting joyfully in the midst of the medical-school literature that had struck such despair to the heart of an aspiring journalist. And his freckled face became engulfed by a grin when Larry entered.

He waved a pamphlet hilariously.

"Hello, reporter!" he greeted condescendingly. "What can I do for you today?"

"Hello, Dr. McCleary!" he was answered promptly, whereupon he threw back his shoulders and almost shouted his relief. After re-telling the whole story, he concluded with, "I just came in to tell you that, in the light of recent events, the proper thing for you to do the next time you meet an ant in the garden, is to sidestep and take your cap off to it."

* * * * *

"Larry Goes to the Ant," by Effie Ravenscroft. Published in St. Nicholas, *December 1913. Original text owned by Joe Wheeler. Effie Ravenscroft wrote for popular magazines during the first half of the twentieth century.*

If you've enjoyed reading AMELIA, THE FLYING SQUIRREL, you'll want to read all the books in this remarkable series!

BOOK FIVE: *Spot, the Dog that Broke the Rules and Other Great Heroic Animal Stories*
Paperback, 160 pages
ISBN 13: 978-0-8163-2296-1
ISBN 10: 0-8163-2296-1

BOOK FOUR: *Dick, the Babysitting Bear and Other Great Wild Animal Stories*
Paperback, 160 pages
ISBN 13: 978-0-8163-2221-3
ISBN 10: 0-8163-2221-X

BOOK THREE: *Wildfire, the Red Stallion and Other Great Horse Stories*
Paperback, 160 pages
ISBN 13: 978-0-8163-2154-4
ISBN 10: 0-8163-2154-X

BOOK TWO: *Smoky, the Ugliest Cat in the World and Other Great Cat Stories*
Paperback, 160 pages
ISBN 13: 978-0-8163-2121-6
ISBN 10: 0-8163-2121-3

BOOK ONE: *Owney, the Post Office Dog and Other Great Dog Stories*
Paperback, 160 pages
ISBN 13: 978-0-8163-2045-5
ISBN 10: 0-8163-2045-4